Lucy Evangeline Guinness

Across India at the Dawn of the 20th Century

Lucy Evangeline Guinness

Across India at the Dawn of the 20th Century

ISBN/EAN: 9783744696487

Printed in Europe, USA, Canada, Australia, Japan

Cover: Foto ©Andreas Hilbeck / pixelio.de

More available books at **www.hansebooks.com**

Across India

at the Dawn of the 20th Century

By
LUCY E. GUINNESS

London
The Religious Tract Society
56 Paternoster Row and 65 St.
Paul's Churchyard
1898

Preface

ACROSS INDIA the Sun is rising. How deep the shadows lie, how few are the points of illumination still, yet how surely the Light of the world has dawned, and in what ways we may help to bring the coming Everlasting Day, these pages seek to show.

They are very simple pages, glimpses caught in a brief winter visit of three months, commonplace glimpses such as every one sees who has the privilege of visiting our vast Eastern Empire. As a traveller's tale their view is limited — Bombay, Poona, Anantapur, Madras, Calcutta, Darjeeling, Benares, Mirzapur, *voila tout*. But where we did not go in fact, we have since gone in heart, and with the help of Dr. George Smith's *Conversion of India*, of Mr.

PREFACE

Wilder's *Appeal from India*, and of every other Indian missionary book I could obtain, I have tried to bring together leading facts for the whole Empire, and to justify from the missionary standpoint the title *Across India at the Dawn of the 20th Century*.

I have to acknowledge my indebtedness to Dr. George Smith and Mr. Eugene Stock for much valuable help; to the India Office and Home Office for assistance in statistical and educational questions[1]; and to Mr. A. J. Knight for calculating the mathematical mysteries of my diagrams.

For various illustrations my thanks are due to Mr. J. M. Dent, Messrs. Blackwood, Mr. Fisher Unwin, the Editor of the *Daily Chronicle*, Dr. George Smith, Mr. W. S. Caine, Mr. T. A. Denny, Bishop Thoburn, Mr. Dyer, Mrs. Menzies, the Church Missionary Society, the Church of Scotland, the Free Church of Scotland, the Bible Society, the Religious Tract Society, the London Missionary Society, the Society for the Suppression of the Opium Traffic, the Sunday School Union, the Zenana Bible and Medical Mission, Miss Woolmer, Miss Spence, Mr. James Lee, Messrs. Bourne & Shepherd of Calcutta, and to Mr. Joseph Walton, M.P.

Above all I am indebted to the Student Volunteer Movement of India and Ceylon for the central message of this book—the survey of unevangelised India, which, summarised and printed on the type maps of Chapters iv., xiv., xvi., and xxi., has been taken from their *Appeal for India*.

As will be seen, Chapter xiv. is written by an abler hand than mine—the dear hand that carried me off unexpectedly to India. That journey, by the way, was unforeseen. On a dull November morning I had come down as usual, expecting the commonplace. The unexpected happened. 'Will you come with me to India?' father said. The question was decided about mid-day. At five o'clock we started. May this book bring to many hearts just such a call to India—a call it may be equally unexpected, a call from a Father's Voice, a call that will mean going, giving, life-labour, and life-prayer.

LUCY E. GUINNESS.

[1] A note will be found with the Index, respecting the statistics employed.

able of Contents

			PAGE
INTRODUCTORY—IN THE ETERNAL CITY			10
CHAPTER I. BOMBAY, THE EYE OF INDIA			17
,, II. BY THE WESTERN SEA			24
,, III. SUN WORSHIPPERS			30
,, IV. DEVOTEES OF EAST AND WEST			35
,, V. PAGES FROM POONA			44
CHAPTER VI. IN A ZENANA BUNGALOW			58
,, VII. THE SHRINES OF POONA			72
,, VIII. RAMABAI			84
,, IX. A LODGE IN THE WILDERNESS			92
,, X. IN A MOFUSSIL MOSQUE			108
,, XI. BY THE EASTERN SEA			120
,, XII. ASSOCIATION WORK—'FROM SHORE TO SHORE'			130
,, XIII. NEO-HINDUISM			138
,, XIV. DOOMED, BUT STILL DOMINANT			146
,, XV. WEDDING AND WIDOWHOOD			157
,, XVI. CALCUTTA AND BENGAL			166
,, XVII. DARJEELING			180
,, XVIII. BETWEEN FOUR HEATHENDOMS			188
,, XIX. THE FOCUS OF HEATHENISM IN INDIA			195
,, XX. WITHIN FOUR WALLS			202
,, XXI. IN THE NORTH-WEST			210
,, XXII. INSIDE A FAMINE POORHOUSE			222
,, XXIII. THE RIVERS OF THE UNWATERED LAND			228
,, XXIV. 'RIVERS OF LIVING WATER'			234
,, XXV. 'IF——'			242
,, XXVI. CONCLUSION			250
,, XXVII. THE BEHAR MISSION			254
NOTES			255
INDEX			257

Illustrations

	PAGE
'Carest Thou Not?'	2
The Forum	11
Sculpture from the Arch of Titus—'Judea Capta'	12
Tiara-Bearer to the Pope	13
Sancta Scala	14
The Columbarium	15
Great Native Procession, Bombay	16
The Queen-Empress of India	18
Carvings from the Caves of Elephanta	19
Clock Tower and Secretariat, Bombay	21
Snake Charmers	25
Dr. Mackichan	26
Free Church College, Bombay	27
A Parsee Family at Home	31
Parsee Towers of Silence	33
Walkeshwar	35
Indian Fakirs	36, 37
Self-Torture by Head Burial	38
Indian Devotee sitting on Spikes	41
Weaver at his Loom	45
Road among the Ghauts	46
Sand Map of India	47
Maratha Student	48
John R. Mott	49
John N. Forman	54
R. P. Wilder	54
Young Maratha Brahman	55
Zenana Visiting	59
Poona School Girls	59
Gari and Bible Women	60
Malaysian Girl sewing	61
Women cooking	62
Worshipping Tulsi-tree	65, 66
Dr. Pauline Root	68
Dr. Julia Bissel	68
'At our Mother's knee'	70
Gunputti	72
Golden Temple, Amritsar	73

	PAGE
Hanuman	75
Parvati Temple, Poona	75
Maruti	76
Kali	79
Poona Shrine	81
Ramabai	84
Indian Widow	86
Widows in Ramabai's Home	88
Famine Victims	89
Ramabai's Poona Home	90
Soonderbai Powar and Ramabai	91
Mrs. Hinkley	94
River Scene	95
Street Crowd	96
L.M.S. Mission House, Bellary	97
Bungalow, Malvalli, Mysore	104
Hyderabad	106
Moulvies	113
The Taj Mahal	114, 115
Moslem Pilgrims at the Kaaba	117
Mohammedan Women	118
On the shore, Madras	120
A Jutka	122
Mountains of Travancore	123
Nestorian Tablet, Madras	124
Native Converts, Z.B.M.M.	126
C.M.S. Divinity School, Madras	127
Indian Sunday School Children	129
Christian College, Madras	131
Lord Kinnaird	133

ILLUSTRATIONS

	PAGE
Y.W.C.A. Institute, Calcutta	134
Miss Morley	135
Mrs. E. W. Moore	135
The Misses Kinnaird	136
Bengali Y.W.C.A. Members	137
Head-burial Devotee	140
Hindu Ascetic	142
Poems in Marble	143
Temple Court at Little Conjeeveram	148
Idol-Worship	149
Woman of Travancore	150
Hindu Crowd	151
River Scene, Indore	154
Orissa	155
An Indian Bride	156
A Nine-year-old Wife	159
Indian Bride and Bridegroom	160
A Bride of Eight	160
High-caste Child Wives	163
A Star Photograph	167
The Hooghly, Calcutta	169
Street Scene, Calcutta	170
Post Office, Calcutta	171
General View, Calcutta	173
Dacca	174
William Carey	177
Darjeeling Peasants	180
Thibetan Prayer Wheel	182
Prayer Flags	182
A Dandy	183
Loop on Darjeeling Line	184
Sunrise among the Himalayas	184
Miss Annie Taylor	186
Traders' Encampment at Gnatong	187
Kinchinjanga Range	189
Buddhist Priest	190
Buddhist Temple and Lamas, Darjeeling	191
Festival at Benares	194
Mosque of Aurangzeb, Benares	196
Washing in Ganges	197
Burning Ghats, Benares	198
General View, Benares	199
A Fakir, Benares	200
Gosain Temple, Benares	201
A Fuel Seller	203
Working Girl	203
Rope Makers	204
Women grinding Corn	204, 205
The *Palki-Gari*	207
'Waiting for you'	209
Cawnpore Memorial	211
Sunrise on Mount Everest	213
Himalayan Village God	214
Nanga Parbat	215
Sirrat, in Baltistan	216
Street Scene, Lahore	216
Mountains of Cashmere	218
Street in Lahore	219
Famine Boys	223
A Mirzapur Sufferer	224
In the Mirzapur Poor-house	225
Famine Sufferers	227
Mango Gnsor	228
Godavery Irrigation Works	229
Canal from the Kistna	232
Sir Arthur Cotton	233
'Rivers of Living Water'	234
'Like a River Glorious'	240
Pilgrims entering Mecca	245
Opium Slaves	247
'And He cometh and findeth them asleep'	249
'Our Long Home'	251

Diagrams

DIAGRAM.	AUTHORITY.	PAGE
1. Area of India and habitable globe.	*Conversion of India*, p. 208	18
2. Pop. of India and of globe.	*Statesman's Year Book, Whitaker's Almanack*	18
3. Comp. Populations.	Census Returns	22
4. Average Bombay missionary parish.	Ministers, 39,000. *Statesman's Year Book*, 1898. Missionaries, 291. *Decennial Conference Statistical Abstract*	23
5. Comp. growth of Christianity, Hinduism and Islam.	Beach, Cross and Trident, p. 26	29
6. Indian and British Students.	*Strategic Points in the World's Conquest*, Mott, p. 29. Figures from India Office and Education Department, Whitehall	51
7. Growth of Student Federation.	*Ten Years' Retrospect*, Mott. Report to Williamstown Convention, July, 1897, p. 24	53
8. Non-educated Women and girls.	India *Statistical Abstract*, 1893-4, p. 32	64
9. Woman's parish.	Calcutta *Statistical Tables*, 1890, p. 60	69
10. Hindu Pop. of India comp. with that of United Kingdom.	Broadly speaking five times as great. Hindu Pop., 208,000,000. United Kingdom Pop., 40,000,000	74
11. Comparative Populations.	Mr. Holt Schooling	98
12. India's millions and Missionaries.	*Conversion of India*, p. 144. (Estimate for close of century)	99
13. 60 years' growth Native Christians.	1830, *Conversion of India*, p. 137. 1860, *Statistical Tables*, p. 53. 1890, *Statistical Tables*, pp. 63, 46	100
14. 40 years' growth Communicants, India and Burma.	*Conversion of India*, p. 204	101
15. 42 years' growth Native Ordained Ministry.	*Conversion of India*, p. 206. Calcutta *Statistical Tables*, p. 52	101
16. 20 years' increase Christian Church in India.	*Cross and Trident*, p. 90	102
17. Average parish Hyderabad.	*Statistical Abstract*, '94, p. 1, and *Appeal for India*, Wilder, p. 6	105
18. Moslem Pop. of India.	*Statistical Abstract*, p. 25. 57,000,000	111
19 & 20. Indian Sunday Schools.	Sunday School Union	123, 129
21. Indian Women and Widows.	*Statistical Abstract*, '94, p. 26. (Enlarged estimate)	164
22. Indian Distances.	Stanford	187
23. Pop. Calcutta, etc.	Census Returns	171
24. Growth of Uganda Church.	Church Missionary Society	230
25. Religions of India.	Census Returns	252

Maps

Plan of Bombay City	17	Map of South and Central India	152
Map of Bombay Presidency	42	Map of Bengal	173
Map of Mysore	105	Map of North West India	217
Moslem Map of the World	116	Map of Indian Rivers and Famine	233
Map of Cashmere and Kafiristan	246		

 IN THE ETERNAL

Introductory

'The kingdoms of this world are become the kingdoms of our Lord and of His Christ.'—ST. JOHN

'THE Kingdoms of this world are become the kingdoms of our LORD and of His CHRIST.' One day that word shall sound like a clear trumpet note across the world. And it will be true.

To hasten that day, to help to bring it, in our own hearts and in the hearts of all— for this we live.

* *

If you are going to India or the Far East, and can go by Brindisi, do. Go, if you can, with a week to spare, from Brussels to Bâle, and south through Switzerland and Northern Italy to Venice or Genoa. Spend a night at Milan, and any other nights you can upon the road. See the Italian lakes; see the Duomo and Naples, and, above all, see Rome.

You are starting out, it
may be, for a missionary
life-work. You are going
to face and fight the idolatry
that lives. See, first, the
ruined temples of a dead
idolatry. Realise what has
been.

It shall be.

THE FORUM.

Few things impress one
more in the Eternal City than the traces of a vanished Paganism. The broken statues and ruined halls of the Vestal Virgin's temple, the silence of the Forum, where Cicero's voice rang; the fallen capitals and columns, altars and arches of shrines to Jupiter, Saturn, Venus, and the rest of the old long-dead 'Immortals'; the vast denuded spaces of the Caracalla Baths, once glorious in mosaic and marble; the still triumphant records of Severus', Titus', and Constantine's arches; the soul-stirring memories of the ruined Colosseum; and the appealing silence of the Columbarium — that heathen house of the dead, with the *Vale* of its hopeless inscriptions — all resuscitate the long-vanished world of pagan Rome. One fancies Nero moving through the palace that he built; Marcus Aurelius thinking his great thoughts as he paced beneath his gateway in the city wall— through which we drove in our shabby little modern victoria; the worshippers passing up the Via Sacra between the temples now left desolate; the courts of justice solemnly pronouncing the verdicts of old Roman law, where now glib guides show travellers round the ruins. The athletes wrestling in crowded arenas; the priests serving in silent temples; the white-robed Vestal virgins keeping lonely night vigils by their never-dying fire, or freeing prisoners by a word as they passed in their purity along the streets of Rome; the festivals, the funerals; and, above

all, the actors in the Colosseum tragedies, the cries, the frenzy, the agony, the deaths—all these things live again.

In thought one sees the martyrs stand by those wild beasts' dens, through which you still can walk, surrounded by the lofty tiers of the amphitheatre in their voiceful vacancy. And a wonder and awe fill you as you begin to realise the conquest won by Christ when paganism—this paganism, ancient, cultured, reigning, wealthy, the faith of the world's empire—fell before His cross. The miracle of this overwhelms you. One sees something of what it meant that art, prestige, learning, social custom, a nation's prejudices, as well as all the natural opposition of the heart, should have been arrayed against the martyrs of the Catacombs in vain. It presses in upon you. You feel it was Divine.

Perhaps as much as the sense of a vanished paganism, the presence of a new paganism impresses one at Rome, and the

SCULPTURE FROM THE ARCH OF TITUS—'JUDEA CAPTA.'

SHALL PASS AWAY 13

realization that it too is necessarily destined to pass away. You stand amid the relics of past empires. You see in vision what shall be, the ultimate triumph of the Spiritual.

The Arch of Titus stands close to the Colosseum, recording the whole bygone Jewish system, the story of vanished ages—a world of faith and feeling, national ritual and experience, gone almost as much now as the pagan power before which Judaism fell in the days of Titus.

That pagan power is to-day only a dream lingering among its ruins. And the empire that followed it —what can one say of the

TIARA-BEARER TO THE POPE.

riches of the Vatican, the uninspiring magnificence of St. Peter's, the gorgeous tawdry 'church' interiors with their images and idols, gold and scarlet, tinsel and flowers, candles, curtains, mass performances, costly sculptures, marble pavements, chanting priests, and sacrificing altars? You look and look, and ask yourself a hundred times what possible connection these things have with the teachings of Jesus Christ? The New Testament recurs to you with its simple light, and you stand in silent wonder that a system of this sort could have sprung from such a source.

This was the new Rome that replaced the old, and that is

itself replaced in part already by modern government. We made our little trap stop close to the Palace of the King on the summit of the Quirinal Hill, from which one sees across the city the dome of St. Peter's rising. There they stand, frowning on each other, King and Pope, mutually defiant, each claiming temporal sovereignty. But the temporal power of the Vatican has vanished, as you realise in passing the fine municipal buildings and new law courts which the Government is putting up now at heavy expense, totally ignoring the claims of the Papacy.

Even clearer than the voice of modern Rome in proclaiming the vanishingness of papal empire is the silent utterance of the simple ascent of the Santa Scala.

The marble steps, covered with a wooden case to protect them from the wear of praying knees, rise as they rose when Luther climbed them kneeling, and stopped midway, arrested by the message 'The just shall live by faith.' What an impression the place gives of the triumph of the Spiritual Kingdom! Just as you feel the contrast of the pagan Columbaria with the Christian Catacombs—the one so hopeless, the other so amazing in the confident faith of its dove of peace, palm branches of victory, anchor of hope, and monogram *Icthus* enshrining the name of the Saviour of the world—so at the Santa Scala. In the Catacombs you are conscious of the presence of a new spiritual realm, wholly unknown to that sad pagan *vale in æternum*; and at the Santa Scala in the same way you realise, in contrast to the toilsome works and penances of Rome, the beauty of Christ's kingdom of righteousness, peace, and joy. You stand, so to speak, at the modern birthplace of spiritual liberty. And from that spot the heart goes out to the millions scattered all over the world, whom Jesus has set free. One feels the light and air, the liberty that knows no toil up sacred stairs, no need of priest or mass. One hears a silent death-sentence pronounced on papal Rome.

And from this place you look forth on a missionary life with courage and with confidence in God. The darkness is passing away. Even now the true light shineth. Since the day that Luther knelt here, the Protestant nations of Britain and America have been born. One hundred millions strong, they lead the world. Yet this change, with all its missionary meaning — the hope of heathendom — is but a little stage in the great work of the ages. We are called to take part in it. Slowly it is achieved. One day the ringing trumpet tone will sound its final record — '*The kingdoms of this world are become the kingdoms of our Lord and of His Christ.*'

THE COLUMBARIUM.

GREAT NATIVE PROCESSION, BOMBAY.

Chapter I

BOMBAY, THE EYE OF INDIA

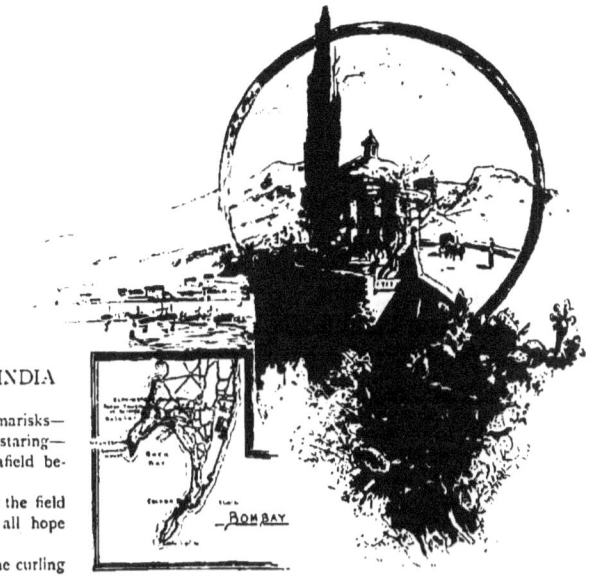

Full day behind the tamarisks—
   the sky is blue and staring—
As the cattle crawl afield beneath the yoke,
And they bear one o'er the field
   path, who is past all hope
   or caring,
To the ghât below the curling
   wreaths of smoke.

    Call on Rama, going slowly, as ye bear a brother lowly—
    Call on Rama, he may hear, perhaps, your voice!
    With our hymn books and our psalters we appeal to other altars,
    And to-day we bid good Christian men rejoice!
KIPLING.

INDIA, India, India! How one falls in love with it! The busy, bright folk—every varied sort and kind; dignified and dirty, richly clad and naked, servile and proud, conjurer and devotee; brilliantly dressed ladies, and gruesome naked beggars protruding deformed limbs,—impossible to count them, describe them, write them down; inevitable to wonder at and love them all!

We have only just landed. Fleeing the hotel, I have found my way down to the beach, and am sitting scribbling to you with the grey incoming tide of Back Bay before me, a few last sunset clouds hanging over the Indian Ocean, and the green heights of Malabar Hill opposite across the water, grey in the fast falling twilight. Parsee priests, venerable in long white flowing garments, and Romanists in black gowns, and all manner of Bombay people, in all manner of costumes, from the habits of the *Mem Sahibs* cantering along the sandy beach, to the scant inches of apron worn by minute brown bairns, pass across this oriental scene, under the evening star, hung far above like a lamp in the cloudless blue.

I am writing now by moonlight. The flame-line along the sea horizon is slowly dying out. The four-faced handsome clock-tower has just struck six, and the great city behind me, ending another hot December day, begins to feel the benediction of the soft, warm evening wind, stealing down the *Maidan*, as they call this sea-front with its grassy links. Stars come out one by one, strange stars that look on India — on the 800,000 of Bombay, lying here rife just now with the plague, and on the 300,000,000 of the Empire, stretching away, away . . . the Empire which, a single land under a single Queen, comprises one-fifteenth of the area of the habitable globe and one-fifth of the human race.

THE QUEEN-EMPRESS OF INDIA.

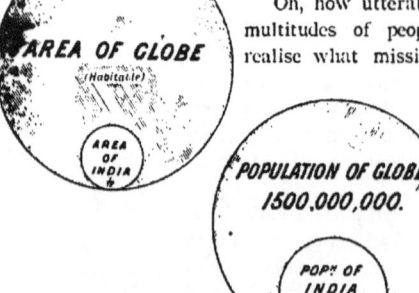

Oh, how utterable it is! These people! These multitudes of people! One begins faintly to realise what missionary work must mean; missionary work, that singular undertaking, which is either the most astoundingly impudent and foolish and hopeless thing in the world, or else the sublimest service which human hands can touch. Think of it for a moment. An hour's steam run from this beach would bring you to the great cave-temple of Elephanta, hewn out 1,000 years ago, and haunted by the memory of centuries of Hindu worship:—

CARVINGS FROM THE CAVES OF ELEPHANTA: MARRIAGE OF SIVA AND PARVATI.

'As the travellers enter its gloomy depths, the desolate silence wraps them round with a heavy, irresistible oppression. So dreary are the shadowy spaces, so hopeless the massive rock-hewn columns, so daunting the immovable weight of the darkly impending roof, that the visitors can hardly rouse themselves to find out what manner of place they are in. . . . With eyes growing used to the darkness they gaze awhile in silence; till the immovable expression of the colossal countenances '—the figures and histories of the Hindu gods carved— 'above them seems to cast a spell on their vague imaginings, and to carry away their minds as captives into a mythic region of ancient fable where the light is more dim, the shadows are more confused than even in the gloomy depths of this abysmal rock-hewn temple.'

Those ancient Hindu fables and the philosophies connected with them have ruled this immense empire for 3,000 years, and to-day rule in India over 200,000,000 minds. Is not the programme of Christianity that lies behind foreign missions astounding? To attack and overthrow the faith thus enshrined for ages, the hoary faith that is the creed of four out of every seven of the inhabitants of the British Empire; that Hinduism which 'terrifies the sinner by its long list of interdictions and punishments—"commit not this or that offence, lest you suffer the torments of awful hells; lest you be born again in some lower condition: kill not, lest you become a dog; steal not, lest you become a rat; restrain your worst appetites and passions, lest you become an impure devil or malignant demon in your next state of existence:"' to substitute for fears like these the love made known by Jesus, is it not sublime service, an end worth living for?

* * * * * *

Yesterday's *Times of India* prints a capital account of Bombay, from an address by Lord Harris, the recent Governor here.

'Imagine,' he says, a 'great city of 800,000 souls lying on the shores of a beautiful sea, glorious in the monsoon, backed by grand mountains with many a castellated peak, nestling in palm groves, with hundreds of sea-going and coasting vessels anchored in its harbour, with two busy lines of railway, with broad thoroughfares, and grand buildings; with a most active and intelligent mercantile community, both European and native; with its lawns crowded day and night with pleasure and leisure seekers, and its brightness added by the most brilliantly dressed ladies in the world, the Parsees. Imagine it if you can; I don't think you can. I have seen many great cities of the East, and I have not seen one that could touch Bombay.

'You know how it became British, as part of the dowry of Catherine of Braganza, who married Charles II. Previous to that, Cromwell had thought of laying hold of it; and in those times our ministers were a little vague as to its whereabouts, for they described it as "near Brazil." And when we took it, it was a poor kind of place indeed; only a scrap of an island, with the sea racing between it and other little islands which have since been connected. Only a little port with a few houses around it, and a population of about 10,000, mostly vagabonds. Pretty unhealthy too, smelling strongly of decaying fish. It killed off seven governors, an ambassador, and an admiral in three years.

'It doesn't sound much of a place to fight for, does it? But we had to, and we did.

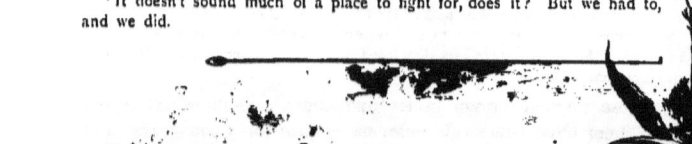

'ON THE SHORES OF A BEAUTIFUL SEA.'

'The Dutch banged at us from the sea, and the Mogul Admiral, the Sidi of Janjira, battered at us; but we clung to it like grim death, sometimes short of men, sometimes of money; pestilence inside, bad times and enemies outside; conscious that as the Tapti silted up and the glory of Surat faded, Bombay, the one great natural commercial harbour of India open to the sea, must become a jewel in the British Crown.

CLOCK TOWER
AND SECRETARIAT,
BOMBAY.

The Secretariat, built at a cost of £130,000, stands next to the University Senate Hall, Library, and Clock Tower, fine buildings designed in French style of the 13th century.

'The cleverest races in India have made it a busy mart; the public-spirited and the philanthropic have spent their money in adorning and endowing it. They have started about 100 cotton-spinning mills, which consume over 3,000,000 cwt. of cotton; and the port of Bombay has a sea-borne trade of about 100 millions of pounds. She has three daily European newspapers and a crowd of weekly vernacular newspapers, a university, several art colleges, a veterinary college, technical and art schools, which latter has turned out most of the masons who have decorated the public buildings. She has boys' and girls' schools in quantities, clubs of all kinds, both native and European, social, yachting, cricket, football, swimming, boating, and golf; three fine volunteer corps, one mounted, one artillery, one rifle—in fact, in every way you can think of, Bombay is as busy as it is possible to be, and in appearance magnificent.

'I may be a little partial, but I really do not know a sight more creditable to British capacity for administration than that of a cricket match on the Parade Ground at Bombay between the Presidency European Eleven and the Parsees. Splendid buildings frame one side of a triangle, the ornate dome of the Railway Terminus almost dwarfed by the size and chaster style of the Municipal Hall, whilst hospitals, colleges, and schools complete the rank. From ten to twenty thousand spectators preserve for themselves an orderly ring, watching with the most intense interest an English game played between Englishmen and natives in a thoroughly good sporting, gentlemanly spirit.

'The motto of Bombay, *Urbs prima in Indis*, is fully justified. Taking into consideration her picturesqueness, position, trade, population, wealth, municipal government, and the activity, education, and natural intelligence of her people,

Bombay is *pucka*, as the Hindustani has it—"quite first class." She has sent over to England the only natives of India who have succeeded in getting into the House of Commons, one as a Liberal and the other as a Conservative, and—still more famous in the athletic world—she sent us the champion batsman for 1896.'

'*Urbs prima!*' mutters my friend here, a magistrate from North India; '*Pucka*, forsooth! If you put that in your book, Miss Guinness, you'll make the Anglo-Indians smile, and certainly offend Calcutta people!'

But my appreciation of Bombay and faith in the good nature of unknown Calcutta folk, is strong enough to accept Lord Harris's panegyric, *pucka* and all.

It is this beautiful city, the second largest in the British Empire after London, and the greatest cotton market in the

Bombay	pop., 822,000	▬▬▬▬▬▬▬
Jamaica	„ 639,000	▬▬▬▬▬
Liverpool	„ 633,000	▬▬▬▬▬

COMPARATIVE POPULATIONS.

world after New Orleans, that is smitten now by plague, eighty or ninety dying every day.

Last night on the hotel verandah we saw a native funeral pass, such a strange picture—warm Indian darkness shrouding the wide boulevard and tropical trees, white electric light flinging heavy shadows on the motley dresses of the passers-by; and then the sudden break of a little group hurrying forward singing as they bear their heavy burden on their shoulders down the road. The dead is wrapped in a simple cloth—no attempt at a coffin, only a gaily-coloured shroud—and goes, accompanied by a strange monotonous song, rather a cry than a song, 'Ram is true! Ram is true! Ram the great is true!' to the burning ghâts by the sea.

We passed them the other evening. Driving along the sea front we came to a long wall, where at a half-open gate a lurid flare of red light struck out across the road. Great fires were burning inside, and wondering what it could be, we stopped to look. It was the burning ghât of the Hindus; a large space, I should think of several acres, with people standing close along the wall (mourners come to see the last of their loved ones), and in the centre an extraordinary vision — great piles of wood

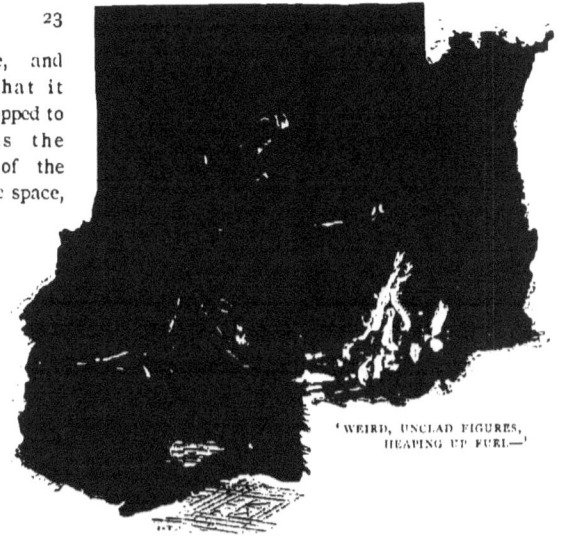

'WEIRD, UNCLAD FIGURES, HEAPING UP FUEL—'

alight and flaming against the black night sky, weird, unclad figures moving darkly among them, heaping up fuel, stirring the fires, and shouting at their work. In each pyre a corpse was being consumed. We stood there for a moment, and then passed out into the quiet darkness under the stars.

'*Rama is true! Rama is true!*' It echoes across India in every Hindu dirge. With a falsehood ringing round them our brothers pass away. What thousands are being carried to these ghâts during the plague! What thousands will be carried there during the next few months! How many of these thousands have died as they have lived, 'without hope, without God!'

Chapter II

BY THE WESTERN SEA

'He must reign till He hath put all enemies under His feet.'

BELOW the wide hotel verandah, when the boats come in —a pretty frequent when at Bombay—oriental magic performs for a few pice. Semi-naked jugglers, conjurers and athletes display their startling stock-in-trade before each new ship's company. Basket tricks, sword tricks, and a score of others, culminating with India's far-famed feat of vanishing, are here done in the open air and on the common road.

Watch this gathering crowd. What a varied medley! 'Africans of many tribes, representatives from nearly every European country, from America, China, and from the islands of the sea' walk these broad boulevards, or stand

*'Gathered to watch some chattering snake-tamer
Wind round his wrist the living jewellery
Of asp and nag, or charm the hooded death
To angry dance with drone of beaded gourd.'*

About a hundred languages, learned books affirm, are spoken in Bombay; but from the officials of the handsome Secretariat, and of the magnificent Post Office, where you call for your home letters, down to the irrepressible pedlar, who incessantly urges curios, smoked spectacles, jewellery, white umbrellas, *topees* and trinkets upon you, all Bombay seems to employ your English mother tongue. The persistent 'boy,' for instance — sketched above in his spotless and tightly-fitting turn-out—the middle-aged 'boy,' who attaches himself to you as a personal attendant, fol-

'—TO WATCH THE CHATTERING SNAKE-TAMER.'

lows you everywhere, and will not be gainsaid, takes the box seat and interprets to the coachman when you drive, deftly waits at table, and stands outside your door anxious to attend to your least wish, brings your afternoon tea unasked, and in a score of skilful ways insinuates himself into your service, speaks English fluently.

There is another Bombay world, of course, but we have scarcely seen it. The great native quarter, ravaged by plague, I am not allowed to visit. The same cause prevents our seeing much of missionary work—schools and colleges are closed and folk away. The day we landed father spoke at the pleasant American M E. Church, and later called on the leaders of the C.M.S., met the newly arrived workers of the Bombay Settlement, British College women come to work for the women of India, and saw the fine Free Church College and Mission House.

Just a day or two's brief glimpse, but it lives in one's memory. Among pleasant Indian pictures that mission house comes back to me. Again we are driving through the balmy darkness of an Indian winter night, driving in an open trap, dressed in summer things, along the moon-lit sea front. The wheels grind crisply on the gravel of a carriage sweep, and stop under the trailing creepers of a wide portico, where in a glow of lamp-light on the dark verandah stands the stately figure of the Free Church College principal. His cordial voice, and the sweet face and motherly kindness of Mrs. Mackichan, welcome us to the first Indian missionary home we have seen. The spacious, airy drawing-room, cool matting and light furniture, the quiet dining-room beyond, with its pretty lamp shades and simply but perfectly appointed table, the pleasant evening meal enriched by the cultured conversation of our host, the chat and music afterwards, Paderewski's music played by the daughters of the house, who have just arrived from their school days at 'home,' the calm of evening worship, the stroll in the garden under the stars by the fine adjoining college buildings, with the music of the sea waves playing just across the road, the kindly farewell wishes and invitation to return—the memory of it all shines in one's thought. And a vista

DR. MACKICHAN.

AT THE GATEWAY

THE FREE CHURCH COLLEGE, BOMBAY.

of far vision opens out in answer to the question, 'Who are these friends? Why here?'

We are standing at the gateway by which Europe enters India. And there has come from Europe to this old world of the East, something immeasurably greater than government, education, commerce, or modern thought; there has come, there is daily coming, the Kingdom of Jesus Christ. Because of the existence of that Kingdom, because of its irresistible power and world-wide destiny, these forces are at work. So far back as 1813 that coming Universal Empire began to reach Bombay. The dry list glows with interest, as you think of what it means:—

Began work in 1813, the Baptist Missionary Society.
,, 1820, the Church Missionary Society.
,, 1823, the Church of Scotland Mission.
,, 1827, the Tract and Book Society and the American Board.
,, 1829, the Free Church Mission.
,, 1834, the Society for the Propagation of the Gospel.

28 'A GRAIN OF MUSTARD SEED

Began work in 1872, the Methodist Episcopal Mission.
  „ 1897, the Bombay Settlement.

Churches for English residents, a pretty Y.M.C.A. centre, Zenana work, medical institutions, Salvation Army barracks, street and bazaar preaching, schools of all sorts, and busy mission presses, are among the active Christian agencies here. And if you look away beyond the city to the Bombay Presidency, another half-dozen good names join the list:—

Began work in 1837, the Basle Missionary Society.
  „ 1840, the Irish Presbyterians.
  „ 1852, the American Presbyterians.
  „ 1860, the Christian Vernacular Education Society
  „ 1865, the Indian Female Normal Schools.
  „ 1893, the Australian Mission.

How many they seem, don't they? But when you recollect that the Bombay Presidency numbers, in the year 1898, 33,000,000 souls, and has only some 300 workers — on an average one Christian worker to about 110,000 of the population—they shrink to their true proportion. Only the fringe of the harvest field is touched here, and the labourers are but few.

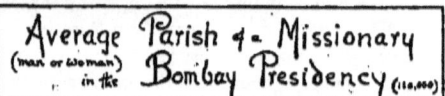

The work is slow and hard. This western seaboard section is one of the most barren of Indian mission fields. It has as yet no record such as that of the Punjab and Telugu churches, with their thousands turned to Christ from idols. But it will have one day. For the plan of which these efforts form part is the great plan of the ages, and the simple Christian forces which we see here at work are 'in the publicly expressed belief, even of purely secular statesmen, destined to develop until they break up the heterogeneous mass of Hinduism, Mohammedanism, and Fetishism,

WHEN IT IS GROWN——' 29

as they did when set in motion by our Lord and His apostles in the heart of the Roman Empire, at Jerusalem and Antioch in the East, at Rome and Spain in the West.'

Already you can see it coming—coming, assuredly coming. Although in this dawnlight of the 20th century, the Christians in India are only 2½ millions among 300 millions, they are increasing twice as fast as the Moslems or Hindus, who outnumber them more than 100 times. They increased twice as fast in the last decade, and will do so with an ever-ascending geometric

ratio, until, like Europe's ancient paganism, Hinduism one day falls with a mighty crash.

'Were the Government of India to do now exactly what Constantine did, the next generation would see more Christians in India than all Europe saw till the final settlement of the northern races in their new seats.' For 'Christianity has introduced a thin wedge into Hinduism which every year's progress is driving farther and farther into the heart of the vast corrupting, cracking mass,' and 'which will, one day, no doubt far distant, but still clearly realisable by faith and common sense, bring all India to the feet of CHRIST.'[1]

[1] Dr. George Smith, *Essays*.

Chapter III
SUN WORSHIPPERS

> Behold, at the door . . . were five and twenty men, with their backs toward the temple of the Lord . . . and they worshipped the sun. . . . Then said he unto me, Hast thou seen this, O son of man?—
> EZEKIEL.

IT is sunset; we are standing on the green heights of Malabar Hill; behind us, stretching out to the horizon, lies the blue Arabian Sea, melting into the Indian Ocean, and washing the western shores of India in a single line of 1,000 miles from this green hill down to Ceylon. Behind us stand the Parsee Towers of Silence, the last home of so many thousand dead. Gay flowers, graceful ferns, and palms, and garden-walks are round us; far below lie the factories and chimneys of Bombay, pretty bungalows half buried in foliage, and out on the harbour vessels and fishing-boats. Warm waves are lapping lazily along the sandy shore.

Close to the tide-edge of the crescent bay, a few yards' space between each man, stands a line of silent worshippers with their backs towards the city and their faces to the sea, praying towards the sinking sun. They are Parsees, Persian in origin, Zoroastrian in faith, despising idolatry, indifferent to Christianity, clever and successful business men. They follow still a faith first preached 3,000 years ago; and for a thousand years have formed in the midst of the Hindus a separate nation, peculiar in race, religion, and social life.

SAVED . . . NOT OF WORKS'

Zoroastrianism explains the old problem of the existence of evil by a very simple theory, *i.e.* that life is governed by two hostile principles, good and evil, which have produced the world. All that is good comes from the former, all that is bad from the latter. The history of the world is the history of their conflict. Such is the general theory. Its practical application brings one back to the old impossible task of saving oneself by good works.

Zoroastrians believe in the immortality of the soul, and in heaven and hell. 'Your good thoughts, good words, and good deeds alone will be your intercessors.' There is a bridge in the Unseen World dividing heaven from hell. After death—

The soul of every man has to give an account of its doings in the past life. Meher Daver, the judge, weighs a man's actions by a scale-pan. If a man's good

A PARSEE FAMILY AT HOME.

actions outweigh his evil ones, even by a small particle, he is allowed to pass over the bridge to heaven. If his evil actions outweigh his good ones, even by a small weight, he is not allowed to pass over the bridge, but is hurled down into the deep abyss of hell. If his good and evil deeds balance each other, he is sent to a place known as Hamast-Gehan, corresponding to the Romish Purgatory and the Mohammedan Aeraf.[1]

Such is the faith of these sun worshippers, or fire worshippers as they are called, from their reverence to fire as the most perfect symbol of the divine glory. Such are the thoughts that fill the minds of the earnest souls among them who, out of the 27,000 Parsees in Bombay, come down to pray where the warm waves wash the quiet shore here every night.

'Save yourself!'—the knell rung out to sin-stained hearts by Romanism, Hinduism, Buddhism, Mohammedanism, is the message of Zoroastrianism too. 'Save yourself!'—the message of every faith except that which proclaims Christ the Saviour.

As yet but few Parsees have come to Him.

'Their prosperity, their energy, and the prospect of advancement,' writes Mr. Wilder in his *Appeal for India*, ' have made many of the younger men materialists. In other cities of the Bombay Presidency and in Feudatory States, there are 29,000—a total for India of 76,000 Parsees. Workers among them should be well educated, and should have a strong personality, to pierce the crust of indifference and worldliness. The ranks of Parseeism are yet unbroken, save in a very few instances.'

At night the darkness of the long *Maidan* is dotted by dozens of glowworm-like lamps set on the ground, and round each a group of Parsee men and lads sit, playing some complicated Indian sort of chess. We spent an evening among them; they seemed perfectly familiar with English, and gave us a cordial welcome, appearing much interested in all that father said. Parsee ladies are well educated, and free to go about just as they choose, but know comparatively little English, as I found on making acquaintance with some on the beach.

The Towers of Silence, close behind us here, look much less dreadful than the Hindu burning ghâts, but are really more repellent, I think. Believing in four sacred elements—earth, water,

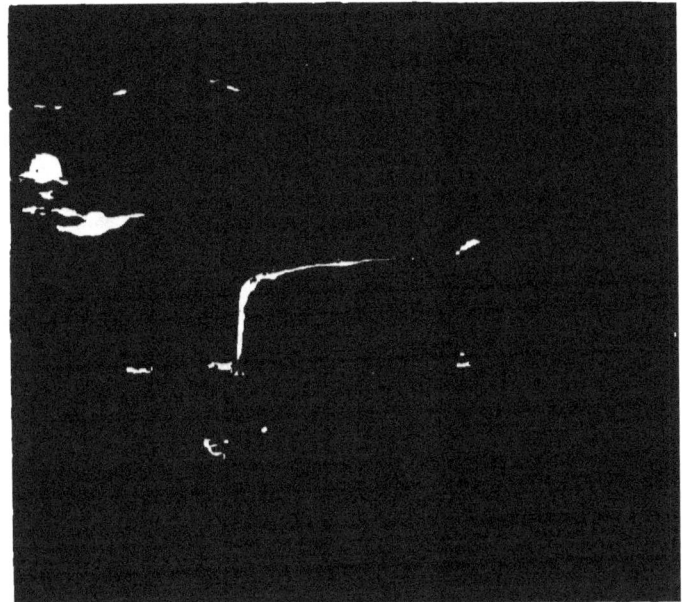

PARSEE TOWERS OF SILENCE, MALABAR HILL, BOMBAY.
(From a painting by the Chevalier Dalton.)

air, and fire—Parsees shrink from tainting any of them by the touch of death, and give their dead in consequence to vultures.

'Amid this lovely garden sloping down to the ocean, five low circular structures of solid granite rise solemnly out of the foliage. Ranged round the summit of these towers, crowded closely together, are rows of loathsome vultures, which, black against the sunset sky, dominate the scene. These birds are still and silent; but when the gate is unlocked for a funeral, they begin to show signs of excitement, which increases as the procession winds slowly up the hill. . . . On reaching the house of prayer, the mourners enter and chant prayers, whilst the corpse-bearers enter the Tower of Silence with the dead body, which they expose naked on the sloping platform invisible to outsiders.

The moment they withdraw, the rows of expectant vultures drop silently down into the tower, and in ten minutes have stripped every particle of flesh off the corpse, reducing it to a bare skeleton before the mourners have finished their prayers. The skeleton remains three or four weeks exposed to the tropical sun, when the bleached bones are reverently placed in a centre well within the tower, where Parsees of high and low degree are left to turn into dust without distinction.'[2]

On a stone slab near the entrance the dead are laid for a last farewell before being carried to the gate. We linger here a little among the flowers, not far from the sacred fire that is never allowed to die. We look from the top of the hill once more on the worshippers along the beach, fastening the sacred cord belt-fashion round them as the sun goes down, and turning home again—old men prostrate on the ground, apparently lost in devotion, slim boys led out to this strange rite, in which no woman joins.

We cannot stay. The picture passes from us as we go down the hill; but the fact lives on. To-night, as the sun rises on Europe, far off across the water, those dark eyes on the sea shore are watching it go down. From these seeking, Christless hearts rises the Zoroastrian prayer.

Chapter IV
DEVOTEES OF EAST AND WEST

A wise and hardy physician will say, *Come out of that,* as the first condition of advice.—EMERSON.

THIS is the holiest place in all Bombay. The picture only shows you a little corner of it—one end of the beautiful tank down to whose clear waters flights of wide shelving steps lead, and where bathers and little children play among reflections of the cloudless skies and picturesque masonry. For the first time we stand within a heathen shrine. It scarcely seems a temple—rather a group of little temples rising among odd buildings, priests' houses, pilgrims' lodgings, native homes. From time immemorial this Tank of Walkeshwar has been a sacred spot. One thinks how many pilgrims have tramped through weary journeys to reach these shining waters, how many anxious, clouded lives have been strained to the utmost to seek what here they seek but never find!

WALKESHWAR.

'STRIVE FOR LIBERATION FROM BIRTH

Four or five of the weirdest *fakirs*, covered with filth and ashes, sit at one end in the hot sun, looking almost more like beasts than men. We could hardly believe our eyes when we saw them—the first *fakirs* we had ever seen—sitting there, almost naked, on the rough ground, surrounded by the various little pots and bowls and odds and ends they employ for life and worship. One or two are smoking a powerful drug which partly stupefies them. One talks to us through an interpreter; another, the most hideous of them all, an animal-looking creature, with masses of matted hair full of dust and ashes, who seems really half insane, makes us a great oration all in his unknown tongue. Louder and louder he talks away, preaching at last at the top of his voice to the little crowd around us, and pausing now and then amid his eloquence to blow shrill blasts on a cow's horn by his side.

'What does he do that for?' we ask our boy.

'Whenever the holy man is hungry he blows his horn, *Mem Sahib*. The people come out then and bring him food.'

What must the faith be whose ideal is before us?

Standing here bewildered in the sunshine, trying to realise that it is not a dream—that to these men, our brothers, this filth, this degradation, this naked idleness, is the embodiment of sanctity—our hearts go out to India, the first glimpse of whose greatest faith meets us in such a form. This is Hinduism, hoary Hinduism, three thousand years old, and ruling to-day more than two hundred million Hindus. And the spectacle before us is the outcome of her teachings!

AN INDIAN FAKIR.

This is the highest thing that you can do. Existence is an

'Hold your arms up till they wither, and the nails grow through the hand.'
AN INDIAN FAKIR.
(*Photographed from life.*)

evil; emancipation from it in this life and in countless future lives is your one hope. Detach yourself from earth—go without clothes; have no home, no friends, no people; do no work; take no interest in anything at all; enjoy nothing, feel nothing, hope for nothing. Detach yourself—to do this, suffer pain; sleep on spikes, starve yourself, or eat carrion and nameless abominations; hold your arms up till they wither, and the nails grow through the hand; do anything and everything to get rid of your supreme curse, conscious existence.

'SLAY THOU THE ENEMY—

DEVOTEE'S SELF-TORTURE BY HEAD BURIAL—A FAKIR AT A FAIR.
(From a photograph.)

'DESIRE' (BHAGAVAD GITA)

It is difficult for us under the influence of JESUS CHRIST to understand and grasp this Hindu theory. To those who know and follow Him CHRIST makes sheer living beautiful, the service of His kingdom here a priceless privilege, and everlasting life beyond the gift of GOD to men. But to the Hindu living without CHRIST—as to some in our own lands who live without Him—mere existence seems a curse.

This poor soul believes himself burdened with being because he is not good enough not to be. Hence he must accumulate merit, raise himself laboriously by weary years of good works, until he can at last escape existence.

'The Hindu devotee,' writes Bishop Thoburn, 'flatters himself that he can by his penances of various kinds accumulate merit. The word penance to his mind conveys no idea of repentance, but solely that of a means of acquiring personal merit. In the next place he is possessed with the idea that matter is inherently evil, and that, since his union with a material body is the source of most of his misfortunes, he must make war on the body in order to liberate the soul. . . . No doubt a large number of both sexes choose a life of asceticism because they find it the simplest and easiest way of securing their daily bread, . . . but many of them show abundant evidence that they are sincere in their purpose, and persist through long lives of severe suffering and privation in faithfully following the course which they have chosen.

'At nearly every great fair a number of men will be seen going through the self-inflicted torture of what is called the "five-fires." Four fires are kept burning constantly around the devotee, while the sun, which makes the fifth, pours down his burning rays upon the head of the sufferer. Others, for months at a time, never allow themselves to lie down to rest, but permit themselves to be supported in a half-reclining position, or sometimes suspended upon a cushion, with their feet dangling down at a distance from the ground. Some sleep on beds made of broken stone, others on spikes; while others again seek torture for the body by abstaining from sleep altogether, or at least reduce their sleeping hours to the narrowest possible limits.'[3]

This nightmare dread of existence is the natural outcome of the transmigration theory, that saddest and most hopeless of all human explanations of life. Did you ever quietly think for one minute what it would mean to believe that everything on the face of the earth was the body of some soul—stocks, and stones, and trees, and rivers; birds, beasts, insects, reptiles, men; mountains, oceans, grains of sand—all alike soul-houses; and that human souls were ceaselessly shifting through countless lives, and must for ever shift, according to their merits or demerits, among these? Think what this faith would mean! Transmigration we call it, and dismiss the idea with a word. But to *believe* that idea, to think that the souls you love best, and that death has called away, are pent up in some body, a jackal's, a cow's, a cabbage's perhaps, and will be bound there, feeling, suffering, enjoying if they can, until death smites them once again, and once again they change their house and pass into some other form as coolies, kings, or what not,—to believe that idea, what must it mean? Think of the burden of it, the endless, restless, weary round, from which is no escape; the grip of Fate that holds you and drives you on and on; the inexorable sentence, from which is no appeal, consigning you to grovelling reptile life or loathsome being. Who knows? You may be born to-morrow a leper, an idiot, a murderer, anything. *Karma*, your fate determines what shall be. And your fate depends entirely on your merits. There is no pity anywhere. There is no forgiveness. Trouble comes to you to-day? Ah, you earned it yesterday, back in your last body. Then you sinned, and you are punished now.

It is so apparently just, this theory. It explains everything—all the crookedness of life, all the strange chance of destiny. It is so hard, so hopeless. Eighty-six million times you will be born and reborn, to suffer, live, and die.

'Let us shorten the eighty-six!' you say.

What more natural? You become a *fakir*. By so doing you detach yourself. You gradually escape reincarnation. You gain a faint and far-off chance of sooner finding rest—the oblivion of Nirvana; not to be.

Standing in this sunshine, looking down on the spectacle before us—on these scarcely human creatures, in their filthiness and ashes, realise the burden of belief that makes them what they are!

THE EIGHTY-SIX!'

'The burden of belief that makes them what they are.
INDIAN DEVOTEE SITTING ON SPIKES.
(*From a photograph*)

And let your heart go out to the Hindus living in the Bombay Presidency only, in this one strip of country along the western coast, a land larger than Spain, running from the frontier of Beluchistan down to the native kingdom of Mysore, and numbering in all 33,000,000 people—district after district, Sind to the north, with the Indus flowing through its sandy plains, and the great port of Kurrachee threatening to rival Bombay, Sind so largely unevangelised; Kutch, by its hot gulf, without a mis-

MAP OF THE Bombay Presidency.
(W. India.)

Showing the Spiritual Needs of a few Leading Districts.

"The harvest truly is great, but the labourers are few: pray ye therefore the Lord of the harvest that He will send forth labourers into His harvest."

SINDH. Men and women missionaries here, all wanted, give only 1 to 125,000 of population. Large districts are unoccupied, and receive only occasional visits from a missionary.

KUTCH. Said to have the population of Uganda, has never had a missionary.

KATHIAWAR — RAJKOTE. 3 missionaries to 1,000,000 people — 1 to 1,000,000. Thousands have never heard of Christ. "I have been these months among a promising people who have never heard the Gospel; who knows when they are likely to hear it again?"

KHANDEISH. 16 Taluks (districts), only 3 occupied. The proportion of Missionaries is 1 to 300,000 people.

AHMEDNUGGAR. Ahmednuggar is a good field, but there are so many Hindus, Mohammedans, and Parsees. A.C.M. has 7 missionaries and 3,000 Christians bat 1,000,000 people.

BOMBAY.

POONA. Pop. 1,067,800. Out of 1,148 towns and villages. 1,135 have no resident Christian and are very rarely visited. Poona itself is well worked, but 1-5ths of the population of the district live in villages largely unreached.

SATARA. Pop. 1¼ millions, area 4,912 sq. m. 1,210 cities, towns and villages. Only 1 male missionary resident, and 2 women workers.

KOLHAPUR. Pop. 1,000,000. 1,293 towns and villages in Ratnagerri district and 1,700 in and near Kolhapur. In but few of these is the Gospel preached even once a year. 3 towns pop. over 10,000, unreached. 16 towns pop. over 5,000, without workers. Thousands of good readers might be reached through the printed page.

BELGAUM. 3 Missionaries to 1,000 people.

In **WADHWAN, GUZERAT,** a Missionary writes:—

"The people listened splendidly. They have never heard before in some cases, in others possibly once." In the Sarat Collectorate "there are hundreds of villages of aboriginal races as reachable as the Fijians were, and with little or no religion to destroy. *In a few years these will have become Brahmanised,* and then work among them will be like knocking our heads against a stone wall. A Government official of one district entreats us to send men there, promising every assistance in his power, and we cannot move. Why? For want of men. We could keep two or three men busy at nothing else than translating and writing. The Bible revision is not expected to be finished in any one's lifetime, and all for lack of men. We have one man to do the work of a minimum of 6 in Surat alone."

sionary; hilly, sea-girt Kathiawar, with but three Christian workers to three millions, a million to a man; and then the mountain country down the long line of the Ghauts, thousands of villages and towns scattered among their heights or on their eastern slopes towards the Deccan; native States, unreached or partly entered, Kolhapur opened by missionary work, Bhor and Phultan unentered, or just beginning to be reached by the new Australian Mission—let the darkness of these people's hearts come to you standing here.

God forbid that the sense of it should ever pass away from us till we have done our part to bring them His 'great light.'

We are looking on the devotees of the Eastern world. Where are the devotees of the West?

Many of them are toiling here in India and scattered in every land. Many are sleeping in distant lonely graves, many working bravely on at home. Are we among their number?

Had we but one-half the devotion to JESUS CHRIST that the *fakirs* before us have to their gloomy faith, should we not do more to reach India's waiting millions? Should we not hasten to give Him our time, our means, our strength, ourselves—to suffer daily loss in that devotion, and to sacrifice, it may be, all that we hold most dear—that we may help to bring these hearts the knowledge of His love?

Chapter V
PAGES FROM POONA

May we never be content with small things. . . . Let us never lose the vision of our possibilities, as with self-denial and prayerfulness we help to realise the plans of GOD.—J. R. MOTT.

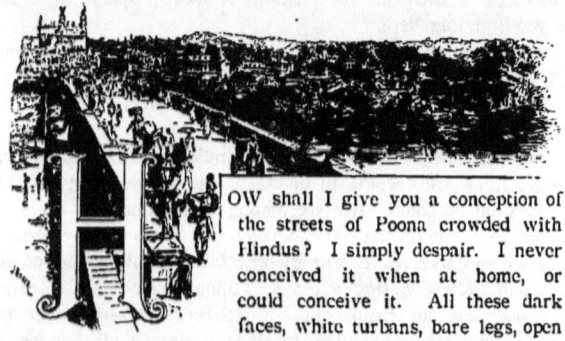

HOW shall I give you a conception of the streets of Poona crowded with Hindus? I simply despair. I never conceived it when at home, or could conceive it. All these dark faces, white turbans, bare legs, open shops; all this movement, crowding, straining; all the dust, the neglect, the unpainted woodwork, the unfurnished rooms, the open-air life, the heat; the strange tongues, the shouting of the drivers as they navigate the narrow, crowded streets, the cataract of souls and bodies,—heathen, heathen, heathen, in fact and aspect. All these temples, so small, towering, dark, repulsive; these priests, these fakirs, these mendicants; this Babel of idolatry, this world of untaught, unholy, unsaved, deluded mortals. Here they are, so real, so helpless, so forgotten!

'Is it earth, or some other planet? We might be in Mercury as far as the heat is concerned—yet this is Christmas Day! The sun blazes in a cloudless firmament, scarce a blade of grass is in the fields. The sunbeams go through you like the emanations of a furnace; you hide from them all the central hours of the day, and only walk abroad in the sweet early morning or starry evening—or if forced abroad at other times go under the protection of a covered conveyance. Where are the snows of winter? Where the fresh breezes of the home hills? Where the rains, the fogs, the frost, and the muddy roads; the fresh air, the cloudy skies, the warm wraps, the winter fires, the closed doors, the whole paraphernalia of indoor and outdoor home life? Not a trace! Another sphere! And yet on the same planet! It seems incredible, yet all most real. Why did we not come before and see it, and feel it, and ponder it, and try to help it? Why? We hardly know. We did not *realise* the truth. We lived in a corner, and called it the world.'

So Father writes, and gives you better than words of mine could, the impression of the novel world in which we are. We move among *the Light of Asia* people—

'THE WEAVER AT HIS LOOM.'

'The traders cross-legged 'mid the spice and grain,
The buyers with their money in the cloth,
The war of words to cheapen this or that,
The shout to clear the road, the huge stone wheels,
The strong slow oxen and their rustling loads,
The singing bearers with the palanquins,
The broad-necked hamals sweating in the sun,
The housewives bearing water from the well
With balanced chatties, and athwart their hips
The black-eyed babes; the fly-swarmed sweetmeat shops,
The weaver at his loom, the cotton-bow
Twanging, the millstones slowly grinding meal. . . .
The blacksmith with a mattock and a spear
Reddening together in his coals, the school
Where round their Guru, in a grave half-moon,
The Sakya children sang the mantras through,
And learned the greater and the lesser gods;
The dyers stretching waist cloths in the sun
Wet from the vats—orange, and rose, and green;
The Brahman proud, the martial Kshatriya,
The humble toiling Sudra——'

Here they all are. Only not 'Sakya children' of that old Benares story, but little urchins of Marathas who usually adopt any imaginable position except that of a 'grave half-moon.'

Indian bairns are so delightful and so odd. If there is anything odder I think it is the housemaid staff of this hotel—where, by the way, we have fallen among Parsees. How I did laugh on arriving in my wee room (which is almost filled by its bed and mosquito curtain) to see, when I turned round from undoing my hat box, no less than six able-bodied men busy housemaiding for me. Two Parsees, three Hindus, and one Englishman were making the bed, and putting on the dressing-cover, apparently quite unconscious of the effect they produced. The room was so small, and they all so busy, officious and polite! There seems to be no woman in the place, except one solitary 'sweeper' who comes round in the morning to the back verandah. But there are numbers of men, all attentive, silent, deferential,—youths, middle-aged men, grey-headed veterans, and one or two bent, decrepit, touching old dears in white frocks and turbans, quite pathetic to watch!

* *

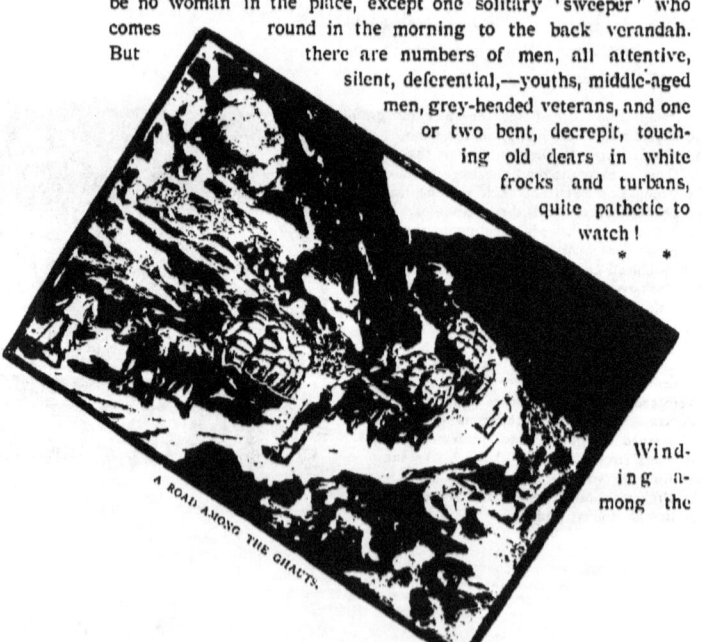

A ROAD AMONG THE GHAUTS.

Winding a-mong the

BUSY HOUSEMAIDING

fine heights of the Western Ghauts, 2,000 feet up from the sea level at Bombay, one of the most beautiful railway lines in the world has brought us to the old capital of the Maratha Kingdom, famed for her warriors 100 years ago, in the days of Warren Hastings. And here amid December heat that makes life tolerable only with open doors and windows, and comfortable only with a *punkah wallah*'s help (*wallah*, by the way, is a delightful word attachable to almost any office, from *gari wallah*—coachman—up to *baby-wallah*), the veil has been lifted for us, in a most pleasant visit of ten days, from two far-reaching sections of mission service. I, staying with Miss Bernard at the Scotch Church Zenana house, am living amid feminine affairs; while Father, at the Wilders', is at the headquarters of work for college men.

Of all sorts of other good things we have had glimpses—of

MAP OF INDIA MADE IN THE SAND AT POONA BY MR. HEYWOOD OF THE C.M.S.

the C.M.S. Divinity School next door, in charge of Mr. and Mrs. Heywood from Bath; of the Australian Mission with its pretty and useful hall; of the dear Salvation Army leaders; the Zenana Bible and Medical Mission, represented here by the active and gifted Sorabji family; the Scotch Church friends — Free and Established — with their excellent schools and hospital; and finally of a whole Conference of earnest American Methodists gathered from Western India to meet our special friends, Bishop and Mrs. Thoburn.

All these we have seen, and I would try to tell you about them if such things had not been often better told before. Two efforts, however, we have had time to study, and of them I 'cannot but speak.'

* * *

A MARATHA STUDENT.

A crowded noisy street outside; within, a lamp-lit, low-roofed stage, a sense of gloom, heat, darkness; and beyond the line where footlights ought to be, a cavernous hall, brightened by white or gaily-coloured gowns of Hindu students—dark faces and gay turbans in a dim, flickering light.

We are in the Poona native theatre, the oddest place, big, ramshackled, dirty, with air and daylight coming in through great holes in the roof, two galleries supported by roughly-cut wooden pillars, the whole dimly illuminated by candles hung high up in big glass bowls. Hundreds of men,

AND ITS WIDE INFLUENCE 49

mostly young students, are there; no women among them. Custom prohibits feminine folk from attending general meetings.

We are face to face with a section of the student world of India, the 16,000 young men studying at this moment in Indian colleges granting the B.A. or some professional degree, and the 70,000 students of the two highest classes of High Schools. Besides these men in training India has tens of thousands of young fellows who have passed through college, so that these intelligent faces represent a great and growing company.

Statistics show that over 20,000 Indian college men passed entrance examinations in the ten years ending 1882-3. Between 1881 and 1891 they increased to over 40,000. The number taking the B.A. degree alone in the ten years ending 1882-3 was 2,391. In the decade ending 1890-1 it had increased to 7,159.

These figures, compared with those of the United Kingdom, are well worth thoughtful notice. We have as many university students in India as at home.

As Sir Charles Aitchison remarked:—' We are rapidly raising up in India a class of men as highly educated and cultured as the generality of the young men who leave the schools and colleges of England . . . men of the press and of the pen; writers of native literature; with whom rests the control of the destinies of India. Their influence whether for good or bad is very great, and must be increasingly felt.'

Nearly all the most important positions in the Civil Service, which are open to Indians, are filled by students.

JOHN R. MOTT.

'In attending the Indian National Congress,' writes Mr. John R. Mott, 'I was impressed by the large number of delegates holding university degrees. More and more India will be governed, and its thought-life moulded, by the student class. The burning question is, Shall this leadership be heathen, agnostic, or Christian? It certainly will not be Christian unless there be in the present generation a great increase in the number of Christian workers among students.'

What faith shall the students of India hold? This question is one of the gravest that India has to meet. The day has long since gone by in which we might expect the influence of her leaders to be that of the old *régime*. With fourteen million readers, and a million added every year; with 153,000 Educational Institutions; four and a half million students at primary schools examined by Government inspectors; and 17,000 College Students; with 6,000 volumes pouring every year from her press, and an annual college and university output of 2,000 educated young men—1380 B.A.s in 1897—India is fast leaving behind her the days when Macaulay described her learning as 'medical doctrines which would disgrace an English farrier, astronomy which would move laughter in girls at an English boarding-school, history abounding in kings thirty feet high and reigns thirty thousand years long, and geography made of seas of treacle and oceans of butter.'

But what shall take the place of the old abandoned notions?

As we look across the footlights into this dim theatre pit, we feel part of the answer is before us. For what has brought us here to-night? The Student Volunteer Movement of India and Ceylon, an organisation as wide as the Indian Empire in its scope; as lofty in its standards as the teachings of Jesus Christ. In 1896-7 its leaders held in eleven weeks, five young men's conferences in important centres—conferences attended by men representing a larger number of educational institutions than were represented that year at the student gatherings of Great Britain, Germany, Scandinavia, and Switzerland combined. Nearly all the sixty Missionary Societies at work in India were represented, over 300 missionaries attending, among them many of the foremost educationalists of the country. The subjoined

Students of East and West

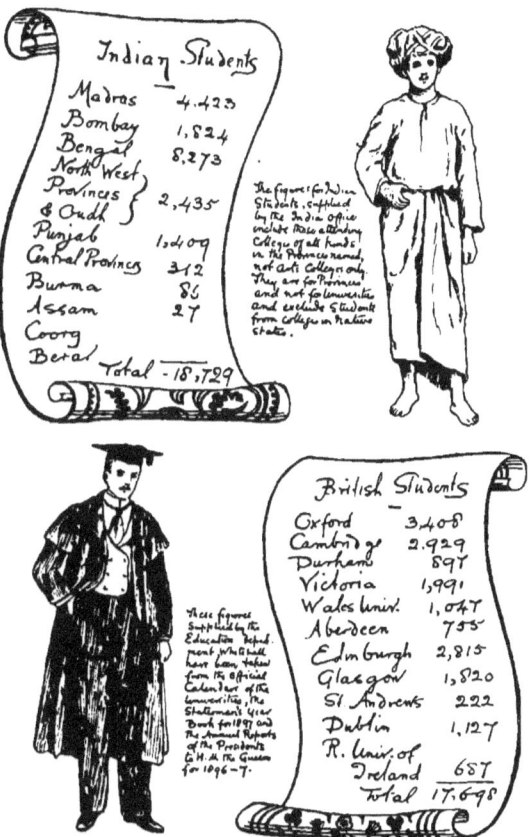

NOTE.—The above figures approximately represent the number of Students at Universities in the United Kingdom. The London University, which is only an examining body, and has no resident students and no teaching staff, is not included in the list.

table shows the significance of this movement among College men.

	Bombay	Lahore	Lucknow	Calcutta	Madras	Total
Number of schools and colleges represented	20	18	22	25	35	120
,, student delegates	75	100	127	157	300	759
,, missionary societies	21	9	12	27	19	52
,, missionaries present	50	60	58	78	65	311
,, other workers	25	50	5	5	35	120
Total number of delegates	150	210	190	240	400	1190
Number accepting Christ	5	15	20	4	32	76
,, volunteering	4	21	29	31	42	127
,, deciding to keep the Morning Watch	35	157	114	101	170	577

'We have the names,' writes Mr. Mott, 'of 127 student delegates who at these conferences decided to devote their whole lives to Christian work in India. No pressure was brought to bear upon them save that of the Holy Spirit speaking through the Word of GOD, and the spiritual needs of India. Emphatic testimony was repeatedly borne by the missionaries to the ability and character of these volunteers. In India, in a special degree, the inducements are great to lead students to enter distinctively secular pursuits. This splendid offering of men constitutes the vanguard of a Student Volunteer Movement for India.

'After counting the cost, 577 delegates entered into covenant to keep the Morning Watch. This signifies their purpose to devote not less than half an hour at the beginning of each day to devotional Bible study and communion with God. Their names were placed in the hands of leading workers at different centres, who will see that they are guided and encouraged in carrying out this resolution. This result will be a cause of greater things; because it is the very opening of the channels of life and power.

'Seventy-six students for the first time accepted Jesus Christ as a personal Saviour. A much larger number who had wandered from Him returned to their allegiance. Among the number who took this stand were not only agnostics, but also Hindus, Mohammedans, and Buddhists. In no country have I seen students accept Christ with greater intelligence, with more purpose of heart, or in the face of so great difficulties.'

To-night's meeting does not stand alone. It is part of a world-wide movement, born only recently[4] but now a potent factor in College life of East and West. At Oxford and

IN INDIA 53

Ten Years' Growth
STUDENT CHRISTIAN MOVEMENT

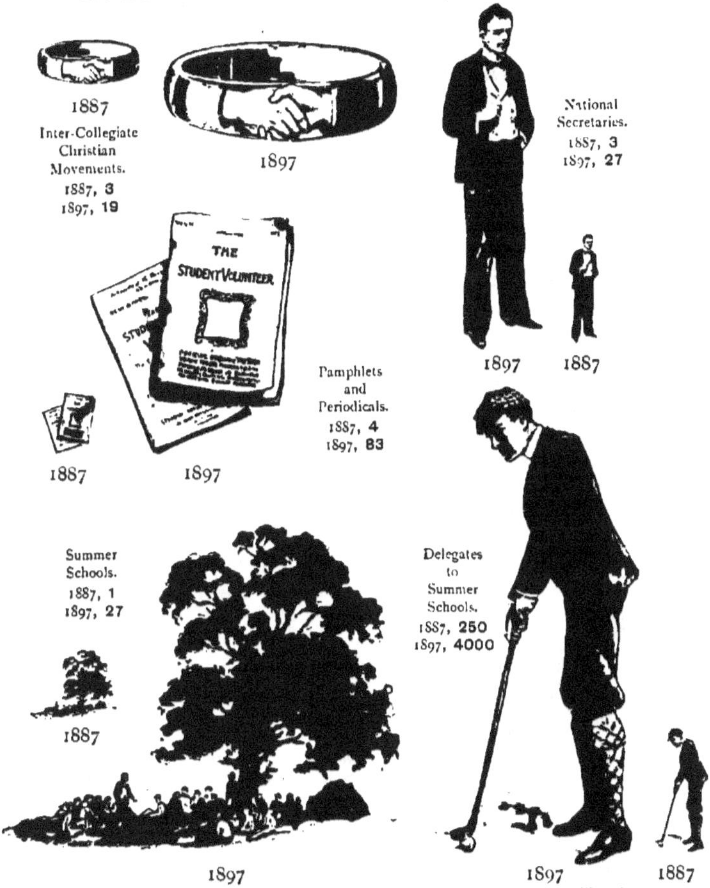

Inter-Collegiate Christian Movements.
1887, **3**
1897, **19**

1887 1897

Pamphlets and Periodicals.
1887, **4**
1897, **83**

1887 1897

National Secretaries.
1887, **3**
1897, **27**

1897 1887

Summer Schools.
1887, **1**
1897, **27**

Delegates to Summer Schools.
1887, **250**
1897, **4000**

1887

1897 1897 1887

[See *A Ten Years' Retrospect*, General Secretary's *Report* to the Williamstown Convention, WORLD'S STUDENT CHRISTIAN FEDERATION, July, 1897.]

Cambridge, Edinburgh and Dublin, in Yale and Harvard, Wellesley and Girton, Newnham and Mount Holyoak, in university halls and class-rooms as different and as far apart as Pekin and Chicago, Calcutta and Durban, Melbourne and Yokohama, Constantinople and Honolulu, thousands of student meetings such as this have, during the last decade, caught inspiration from the risen Christ. Thousands of men and women have gone from them to dedicate their lives to His service anywhere. Already recording five general conventions, held in America and England, the movement

JOHN N. FORMAN.
One of the first S.V.M. Travelling Secretaries.

gathers its Summer Schools every year on both sides of the Atlantic, linking in a single brotherhood—THE WORLD'S STUDENT CHRISTIAN FEDERATION—men and women of America, Great Britain and Ireland, Germany, France, Scandinavia, India and Ceylon, Australia and New Zealand, South Africa, China and Japan. And this for no May-day pleasuring, but for a higher, holier life, for the self-sacrifice and service of following Jesus Christ.

To obey Him many a Western student must forsake home, friends, all the world calls 'success in life,' and must, uprooted from his native land, go as Christ's messenger to exile, a foreign language, weary toil, and in some lands to severe physical suffering. In the East to join this brotherhood means often what is harder. A young Brahman, once Hindu and now Christian, one of the firstfruits of the Poona student work, is here to-night. Of the persecution he has had to bear Mr. Wilder writes:—

'After baptism, Govind tore off his sacred thread—laying aside his caste. After a lecture, Govind appeared and begged the privilege of addressing the Brahmins. He spoke with wonderful courage: "Christ had saved me. I am ready to die for Him. You can do what you wish to me."

R. P. WILDER.
S.V.M.U. India and Ceylon.

'It was like throwing a lighted match into a powder magazine. One kicked him, and another went to the length of spitting in his face. Poor Govind was weeping, and on my asking him the reason, came the reply, "I do not mind their kicking me, but it was hard to have them spit in my face." I told him that our Lord was thus treated, "And they spat upon Him, and took the reeds and smote Him on the head." Two Brahmin students then appeared. One said to Govind,—

'"You did right."

'Another said to me, "You must be glad to see the fruit of your preaching. More may be converted. I am ready to be, if convinced."

A YOUNG MARATHA BRAHMAN.

'During singing in our rooms one cried out in honour of the god Gumpati. He was promptly removed. Then there was comparative quiet inside, but a large crowd gathered outside. I went down and spoke to them, and quieted them somewhat.

'A student brought me his Bible and said, "Keep it, please; the crowd down on the street is tearing up Bibles after snatching them from the members of the class. They will tear mine unless you take charge of it." I put his Bible in my bag, the lights were extinguished, the door locked. As I was feeling my way down the stairs, a Brahmin inquirer whispered, "Be careful, Mr. Wilder." It was sweet to have his friendship at such a trying time, even though he was so timid. On reaching the street, I went up to the crowd, remarking that there was a larger number outside than in, and asking the meaning of the gathering. One said,—

'"We are advising all students to keep away from your rooms. It is our duty to do so."

'I replied, "None need come if unwilling to come. At the beginning of our work we said so, did we not?"

'"Yes," was the reply. Then a student pushed another into me, and something about the size of a croquet ball flew past my face. Then I spoke to the crowd:—

'"You are nothing new. For 1,800 years Christians have been persecuted. We rejoice that we are counted worthy to suffer dishonour for Christ's sake. If your purpose is to persecute us, do so. We are ready and willing."

'They were quiet while I spoke, and I believe one said, "We have nothing against you." As we went to our *tonga* (carriage), one cried, "Break the *tonga*"; another threw a stone against the *tonga*, and we drove home. Of course, we know not what will take place. Pray for us, that we may be constantly filled with the Holy Spirit and speak God's Word with boldness.'

Our thoughts have travelled far while the motley audience gathers. Now with a few words of prayer the lecture opens and Father rises to speak. He has addressed these men, in English, for five nights on a series of great subjects—the Bible, the Jews, the Gospel, the Kingdom of God. Whenever he touches upon idolatry the audience grows restless. Anger and opposition are not far away. But by avoiding direct attack on heathenism one can preach the Gospel and open out the shining sphere of Christian truth unhindered, indeed welcomed. As to-night he speaks on the greatest theme of all, Jesus Christ, His—

Conquest of Heathenism in the Roman Empire—300 years' struggle;
Conquest of Greek philosophy and culture;
Position between Judaism and Christianity, the goal of the one, the starting-point of the other;
Incomparable character, contrasted with the greatest human lives;
Sinlessness, contrasted with the highest saints of all time;
Transforming influence on earth—a moral miracle;

—a conception of the transcendent glory of the Saviour seems to dawn upon the audience. Watching the rivetted faces of the men, leaning against the rough wood pillars or standing in the aisle, and the dark eyes in the benches of the pit fixed on the speaker —educated, intelligent minds behind them that yet sincerely believe in the whole impossible pantheon of Hindu divinities, Siva, Krishna, Kali, and the rest, and seriously defend idol worship— one realises what Jesus has accomplished for us, for the world, for Jew and Greek and Roman, what He will yet do for India's millions.

With one of those flashes of illuminating insight, which in a single moment more than recompense long years of painful toil, one sees the divine plan and the supernatural forces in the midst of which we stand. This bond of Christian brotherhood springing up in India for the first time in the ages, and calling out from her intellectual centres an offering of strong young life to the service of Jesus Christ—this brotherhood binding to purity and love the flower of student life throughout the world—is but one more of the works of Christ; one more part of His eternal Whole. The thought of that Whole, the fact of it, shines on the inner vision—beautiful and wonderful and clear and large and sweet—like all God's things, God's plans that cannot fail, God's springtimes and His life-gifts—natural, inevitable, irresistible; a stage in the coming new creation; His rising light that cannot be put out.

*   *   *   *   *

With a solemn appeal for self-consecration to Christ the lecture closes. Silence falls on the shadowy hall. As a rule the men leave hastily, but to-night something seems to hold them spellbound. There is the hush of a spiritual Presence, a sense of the Unseen, of the reality, the majesty and the claims of Jesus Christ that most around us, probably, have never felt before, but that has reached their hearts to-night—God grant to bear eternal fruit!

Chapter VI
IN A ZENANA BUNGALOW

What's the matter with this country is not in the least political, but an all-round entanglement of physical, social, and moral evils and corruptions, all, more or less, due to the unnatural treatment of women. You can't gather figs from thistles, and so long as the system of infant marriage, the prohibition of the re-marriage of widows, the life-long imprisonment of wives, in a worse than penal confinement, and the withholding from them of any kind of education or treatment as rational beings continues, the country cannot advance a step. Half of it is morally dead, and worse than dead, that is just the half from which we have a right to look for the best impulses. It is right here where the trouble is, and not in any political considerations whatsoever. The foundations of their life are rotten—utterly rotten. . . . The men talk of their rights and privileges. I have seen the women that bear these very men, and again—may God forgive the men.—RUDYARD KIPLING.

A TALL AND SOLEMN NATIVE
GENTLEMAN.

I AM just come in from an interview with my dressmaker—a tall and solemn native gentleman in a red turban and white gown of singular mechanism, who nods his head from side to side and utters deep-toned, incomprehensible monosyllables when one tells him (by interpretation) to put more fulness in the front of one's blouse. He is extremely dignified and stately, with a furrowed brown-skinned face, and noble bearing, and he makes you a frock for four rupees—about 5s.

I lay hold of him as the last and therefore uppermost object in this world of novel, startling objects and sensations—lay hold of him as something to capture for you, out of the sea of strange impressions that makes me almost despair of ever telling you one-thousandth part of

TO BE THERE!

what we see and feel.

Can you see and feel it with me? Can you fancy yourself snatched away from foggy little England, waking one Christmas morning amid the calm of a zenana bungalow? Sunshine and balmy air float in through open windows, and you sit down in muslin under the pleasant *tatti* shade to your *chota hazari*,[1] watching the sleepy white bullocks tethered to the tree across the sunny yard, lazily lift themselves to get their

THREE OF MISS BERNARD'S POONA GIRLS.

morning meal, armfuls of hay stuff thrown down by their bare-legged brown-skinned *wallah*—I really cannot grasp her proper name. And from that morning hour on through the pleasant day can you fancy yourself sharing, as I am sharing now through

VISITING.

Miss Bernard's motherly hospitality, the sweet and simple home-life of a mission bungalow—the cool verandah almost hidden by graceful creepers, through which delicious lights and shadows fall; the hush of the morning hour, with its soft rise and fall of voices in the south porch, where the *munshi* is giving language lessons; the bright and friendly meal-times; the New Year's Day excursion of the native girls' school, with its games and songs and simple feast out by the river side; and then the busy work times, the capital town classes of large-eyed, meek-faced girls, bright boys, and oddest chubby 'infants';

[1] 'Little breakfast.'

the village schools, held in the open air, the zenana visiting from house to house in city streets and courtyards, where you and all the women sit down on the unfurnished floor, and the gossips from next door drop in to listen, men being, of course, forbidden entrance. I wish you could see it, and, above all, feel the atmosphere of loving prayer and simple faith in which the workers move.

Such is life in this *friedenheim*, the zenana house of the Church of Scotland Poona Mission, whose three departments are under three devoted sisters, Miss Bernard here, her sister just across the road carrying on the Girls' School, and Dr. Bernard in charge of the women's hospital, in whose bright wards we found among the nurses Miss Williams, one of our deaconesses from far-away East London. Such is this home of peace, where, when the Bible women come on Sunday morning, the *gari* waits at the verandah steps for a few moments before the day's work begins, while, standing at the wide and ever-open doorway, Indian and English-women join in prayer. In this spirit, in this fellowship, and in the love and labour of which it is the secret, the happy days go by.

* * *

Only yesterday, so to speak, only on the last page of India's story, a home like this was utterly unknown throughout all India. Four unmarried women living alone as religious teachers—who could have dreamt of such a thing before the English came, in the days when 'the heir of

BIBLE WOMEN AND GARI.

Sevajee, a *roi fainéant*, chewed bang and toyed with dancing girls in a State prison at Sattara, while his Peshwa, or mayor of the palace, a great hereditary magistrate, whose authority was obeyed in spacious provinces, held his court with kingly state at Poona' here? Women throughout the Eastern world lived their simple lives, toiled at their cooking and household work as their mothers had done before them, loved and suffered and passed away, without dreaming that a wider existence could ever open to them, existence enriched by mental culture, social freedom, and above all by the highest relationship — heart union even now and here amid common work, with God.

'WOMEN THROUGHOUT THE EASTERN WORLD DID AS THEIR MOTHERS HAD DONE.'

For the customs of India, the outcome of its faiths, have for ages deprived women of education, freedom of thought and action, and of social equality with man.

'A woman is never fit for independence,' writes the great law-

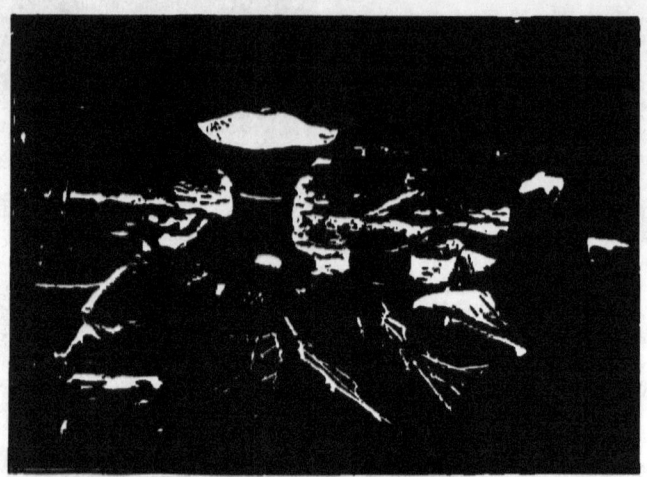

'TOILED AT THEIR COOKING AND HOUSEHOLD WORK.'

giver, Manu. . . . For women no sacramental rite is performed . . . destitute of strength, and destitute of knowledge of Vedic texts, women are as impure as falsehood itself; that is a fixed rule' (Manu, ix. 10-18).

This incredible opinion shows itself in social customs. The Indian wife must rise and stand in her husband's presence. She must leave the room if any other man appears. 'She is forbidden to read the sacred Scriptures, and has no right to pronounce a single syllable out of them. . . . She is never to be trusted, matters of importance are never to be committed to her.' The Indian home has no family table. The women take their meals after the men, and 'the wife as a rule eats what her lord may please to leave on his plate.' Although

WOMEN FOLK!

no law has ever said so, 'the popular belief is that a woman can have no salvation unless she be formally married.'

It is difficult, indeed, to imagine how people holding views like these must regard unmarried missionary women living alone, acting as religious and secular teachers, and managing extensive household and mission matters without the smallest help from any man! And how noteworthy the fact is that women such as these are the product of no faith except Christianity. Hinduism has its temple women—abandoned for life to depravity in the name of religion. Buddhism has its nuns—secluded from the world to secure their own salvation. No faith but that of Christ has ever produced women like the inmates of this zenana bungalow.

They are unmarried truly, but they are not under vows of celibacy. There can arise, there often have arisen in that singular domain the mind of man, schemes of existence centering round some sweet missionary girl, theories of life sufficiently daring to contemplate arresting this white-robed Englishwoman in the midst of her self-possessed and self-directing ways, appropriating and transferring her sweetness otherwhere. Letters proposing revolutions such as these find their way to zenana bungalows as surely as they do to other houses, with, I believe, the happiest results. There can arise, there often have arisen, in that wide and shining dreamland, the thoughts of woman, visions of the beauty of creating another home, the sound of voices calling—dream voices, tender voices—to whose claim even missionary women feel they must respond.

But in passing from the one home to the other, the true

zenana worker carries the old love, faith purposes and mission, and lives as much as she lived before—though her feet tread different paths—'to do the will of Him that sent her,' and 'to finish His work.' She is for ever conscious that she belongs to God, and that He entrusts her not only with the duties that spring from earthly love, but with a solemn wider charge, the charge that comes from knowing His great redeeming purposes, while to one-half the world they are unknown. Beside the beloved presence that has transformed her life, she is conscious of the presence of India's girls and women—145 million hearts just like her own, but scarcely any of them living the free life she lives, because so few among them know the Christ who sets us free. Millions of these women are shut up in zenanas because they cannot be trusted with common liberty; because the men of India have not been taught by Christ to honour womanhood unselfishly. Over 144 millions of them can neither read nor write, and are not under any instruction. Something has come into this woman's life that constrains her to try and

DIAGRAM SHOWING THE NUMBER OF INDIA'S GIRLS AND WOMEN—145 MILLIONS.

Each black leaf represents ⅓ of a million; the three shaded leaves represent the women and girls who can read or are under instruction.

help these long neglected millions. She must, she cannot help it, if she be true to Christ.

Have not you, too, felt that great compelling power? Have you ever thought of where it is leading you, if you faithfully follow on?

Belonging as we do to Jesus Christ, pledged by vows of consecration to His service, are not we women profoundly concerned in the fact that there is no greater hindrance to the coming of His Kingdom in India than India's women—women whom we alone can reach?

'Woman,' writes Dr. George Smith, 'because she is ignorant, is the greatest obstacle to the progress of the Gospel in India. She has no intellect to exercise, no hopes or fears, no amusements, or variety in her monotonous life, but the legends, the ceremonies, and the great periodical festivals of Hindu idolatry. To her, immured in the female apartments, idolatry is all in all; destroy it, and there is desolation in her heart. The picture of Micah, the man of Mount Ephraim, and his mother, in the Book of Judges, is a vivid representation of Hindu life—the mother's curses of her son who took the silver meant for the fashioning of idols, her blessings when it was restored —"I had wholly dedicated the silver to the Lord from my hand for my son"; the "house of gods," the ephod and Teraphim, and the consecration of Micah's son again as priest; and finally, the bitter cry when the idols were stolen—"Ye have taken away my gods which I made, and the priest; and what have I more?" Take away her idols, and the cry of every one of the 145,000,000 females under our rule in India will be—What have I more? It is yours, it is the duty and privilege of every

HINDU WOMAN BRINGING OFFERINGS TO THE TULSI TREE.

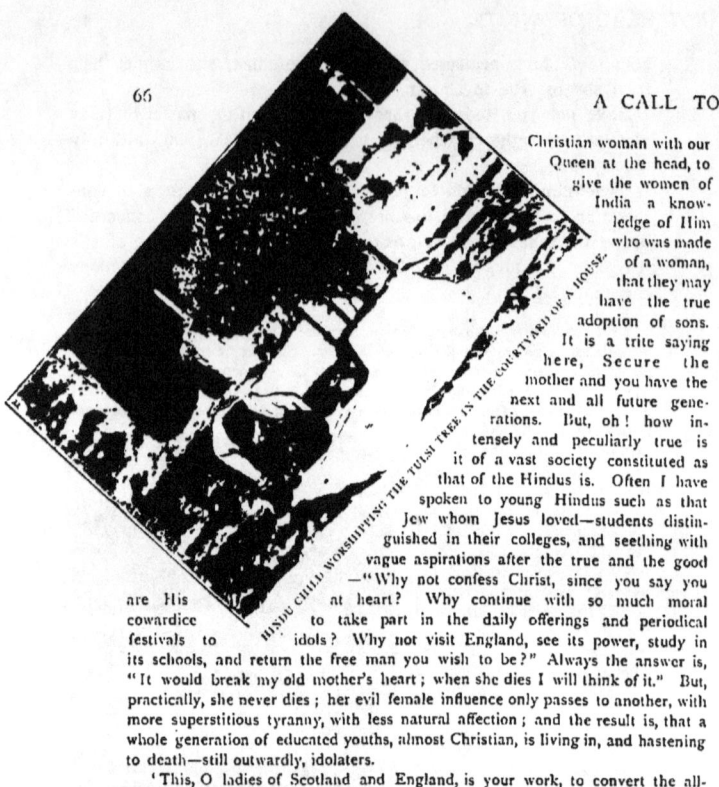

HINDU CHILD WORSHIPPING THE TULSI TREE IN THE COURTYARD OF A HOUSE.

Christian woman with our Queen at the head, to give the women of India a knowledge of Him who was made of a woman, that they may have the true adoption of sons. It is a trite saying here, Secure the mother and you have the next and all future generations. But, oh! how intensely and peculiarly true is it of a vast society constituted as that of the Hindus is. Often I have spoken to young Hindus such as that Jew whom Jesus loved—students distinguished in their colleges, and seething with vague aspirations after the true and the good —"Why not confess Christ, since you say you are His at heart? Why continue with so much moral cowardice to take part in the daily offerings and periodical festivals to idols? Why not visit England, see its power, study in its schools, and return the free man you wish to be?" Always the answer is, "It would break my old mother's heart; when she dies I will think of it." But, practically, she never dies; her evil female influence only passes to another, with more superstitious tyranny, with less natural affection; and the result is, that a whole generation of educated youths, almost Christian, is living in, and hastening to death—still outwardly, idolaters.

'This, O ladies of Scotland and England, is your work, to convert the all-powerful influence of woman from the greatest obstacle into the most efficient aid in the great march of Indian progress. Till you do so, all the education of the men becomes to some extent a curse, by widening the gap between the sexes, and driving the enlightened youths of India from the stupid dulness of their own homes to the haunts of the professionally abandoned *heterœ*, who, in the modern as in the ancient heathen world, are the best educated and most polished of their sex. . . .

'Many young ladies, members of your society, or friends under your private influence, every year go out to India married, or to be married. Accustomed to the active work of Christian benevolence here—to Sabbath schools, district visiting, the comforting of the bereaved, and the succour of the poor—such ladies complain that, in the solitude of an Indian station, and the lassitude of a tropical clime, they have nothing to do, nothing to renew old memories of holy work, no practical duty to keep the flame of personal piety burning in their breast. Indian *ennui* or *heimweh* seizes them, as it seizes only the idle and despondent, and they blame a land where every human being they meet, every idol house they see, cries to them for active care. . . .

'If every Christian English lady in India devoted only one hour a week to the establishment and superintendence of a female school in her vicinity, whether in the city zenana or in the village hut, we should be able to say with more certainty than at present, the redemption of India draweth nigh.'

Eight years ago when the last count was made, over 700 foreign and Eurasian Christian women were at work in India for Indian women. They were then directing more than 300 native Bible women, teaching over seventy thousand children, and visiting more than thirty-two thousand shut-in zenana pupils. Their work, divided according to the Societies they represent, is shown on these eight little flags.

Among them were fifty lady doctors, nearly all in charge of hospitals or dispensaries, a few of them independent practitioners, but none the less doing genuine missionary work—just such work as might be done by the medical girl-students who read these lines.

American women (like Dr. Julia Bissel of Ahmadnagar, and Dr. Pauline Root of Madura, whose portraits we annex) were the first to step out into this field of noble service, but English Societies have since taken up the work with great enthusiasm, and now have twice as many lady doctors in India.

A mighty spiritual force lies behind all this service. There is no romance about zenana work—daily visitation of ignorant native women, shut up in close small rooms; dull, patient, plodding toil at opening their childish minds to higher

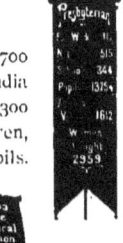

DR. PAULINE ROOT.

things. Nothing but the love of Christ can sustain a person in it.

Results come very slowly. 'If you came often, our hearts would get soft. You only come once a year, we forget,' said a native woman. But how can they go often, if seven or eight hundred of them are to teach one hundred and forty-five millions?

Even the poor women need women workers if they are to be adequately reached; though they mix in the *melas* where evangelistic work is done by men, their husbands do not like them to stand in a crowd to listen. Women must go to them if they are to learn of Christ.

It is otherwise at home. Yet here at home we find special work for women essential. Scores of associations exist in England for nothing but this work. More than 200,000 women are seeking every day to help our women and girls in England, one worker on an average to every fifty or so—a little scrap of a parish represented by the tiny Englishwoman's figure on the accompanying diagram. And this for countries that have had Christianity for ages; while in India, where the first girls' school was opened by Carey only in 1811, the first lady teacher started work in 1823, and the first zenana was not open for visitation till the middle of the nineteenth century, the average parish of each woman worker is 180,000 — represented by the tall figure on the next page.

DR. JULIA BISSEL.

To Christian Women seeking to Help Women

A WOMAN WORKER'S PARISH, IN INDIA AND AT HOME.

THE number of Indian women and girls who want your help compared to those among whom you are working at home is roughly represented by those two women's figures.

In England there are, at a low estimate, 200,000

Christian Women

constantly at work among the 19,000,000 British women and girls. The average parish of each home worker—50 women—is represented by the little figure.

In India there are less than 800

Women Workers

among 145,000,000 women and girls —an average of one worker to 180,000. This average parish of each woman worker in India is represented by the tall figure of a Burmese girl.

'THE MEMORY OF THE THINGS WE LEARNED AT OUR MOTHER'S KNEE.'

How can the womanhood of India be transformed by a force like this? But unless India's women change, India can never rise. For what do we remember best; not sermons, though we have listened to thousands; not the books we have read, though many have made a deep impression on us; at the background of all our thought is a broad life foundation—the memory of the things we learned at our mother's knee.

'If you want to win India,' said one of her leading sons, 'win the women of India. Win the mothers of India, and all India will be Christians.'

I pass on the sentence to the thousands of free, able, unmarried, often unemployed, girls and women living at home, women who belong to the Christ who died for all, and bids us make His great love known 'to every creature.'

'Whoso *keepeth His word*, in him,' in her, 'verily is the love of GOD perfected.'

Chapter VII

THE SHRINES OF POONA

> 'You live with the goddess Shastri! Is she beneficent? Does she tell you secrets of this life and the next, which Science in our West can never understand?'
> 'Who knows more than is known, sahib?' he answered. 'We do as our fathers taught us, and we believe as we were taught; but the goddess is silent, and nobody comes back from the burning ground to say if we are right or wrong.'—SIR EDWIN ARNOLD.

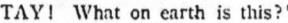

'STAY! What on earth is this?'

We have caught sight, in passing, of a little doll-like object, tricked out in finery, but uglier and odder than any conceivable doll—a preposterous little figure with an elephant's head and trunk attached to a human body, dressed in an immensely full crinoline skirt, and looking like some novel form of elephant ballet-dancer.

'*Mem Sahib*,' replies my guide with the utmost gravity, 'this is the god of wisdom, Gunputti, son of Siva.'

'But why with an elephant's head?'

'Gunputti fought with Vishnu,' answers the *pundit*. 'Siva, to end the quarrel, cut off Gunputti's head. The mother, Kali, threatening to wreck the universe if the head was not restored, Siva promised to do what was needful. But the head could not be found, so he gave him that of the first animal they met—an elephant.'

'An elephant is wise too?'

'Very wise, *Mem Sahib*. Gunputti is invoked by travellers and scholars. His name is written at the head of philosophic books.'

We look at the pantomime doll again—its foolish gown, its ponderous proboscis curling down among the

GUNPUTTI OR GANESA.

THE GOLDEN TEMPLE OF AMRITSAR.

spangles. Yes, it is quite true; India worships this. This is a fair example of her 330,000,000 gods — the gods of Hinduism, that all-inclusive, all-accommodating cult, 'a religion which unites the grossest possible idolatry in the most horrible and degraded forms with a very high development of philosophy; a faith that covers and includes monotheism, polytheism, atheism, morality and immorality, ceremonial, non-ceremonial, no rites or any amount of ritual—binding

DIAGRAM REPRESENTING THE HINDU POPULATION OF INDIA, COMPARED
WITH THE POPULATION OF THE UNITED KINGDOM.

If this picture (3½ inches long) be taken to represent the Hindu population of India (208 millions), the small sketch (⅜ of an inch) would more than represent proportionately the population of the United Kingdom (39 millions).

its followers inflexibly together like columns of the hardest adamantine stone.'

From the Indus and the Ganges to Cape Comorin, and from the Poona shrines we are visiting to-day, away across the continent, till it meets the faith of Buddha in Burmah, the Himalayas and Ceylon, this ancient idolatry still reigns—reigns over more than five times as many men and women as there are in the United Kingdom.

The asceticism of the *fakir* is a slight and single feature of this faith. Self-indulgence, utter license, is a far more frequent form—enshrined, for instance, in Poona's largest temple, Parvati, which, standing on a hill a mile out of the city, overlooks the town and picturesque country, out to the barren mountains beyond the plain, and away to the lake reservoir among the hills. On the roof of that temple tower, with the sun going down in red and golden glory between the hills beyond the lake, we sat and spoke of spiritual things to the guide who showed us over—a talkative, light-hearted, clever creature, trained in a mission school, speaking fluent English, despising idolatry, laughing at Hinduism, and living at the temple by its gains.

With its courtyards, castellated walls and turrets, and numerous varied shrines, Parvati is imposing compared to the common Hindu temples, of which the town is full. Driving along the crowded streets, you see rising here and there behind the houses, pinnacles and horned tower-heads, something like Chinese pagodas; or you meet at the street corners, or under banyan trees, stone hutches, more like dog-kennels than anything else I can think of; wee, odd scraps of things, dozens and dozens of them, about the size of a small fireplace, only roofed in, and square. Sometimes the hutch is four feet high by two or three wide; sometimes merely a small stove-looking affair, solid and square and dirty — always dirty! No, we have seen one exception—an imitation-looking shrine, like a drawing-room ornament, daintily painted with yellow stripes and blue flower work, and a flower-pot on the top; but it was quite unique, and I should think not much used for worship.

PARVATI HILL AND TEMPLE, POONA.

Sometimes the hutch develops into a decent house into which a child might go; often it is larger, and might contain six people; or else, grown into a temple, it has spacious halls and courtyards. But, whatever the size, the contents are unvarying in plan. Maruti, an inconceivably odious object, lives in nearly all the smaller shrines and often in the large. He is the monkey god, a shapeless scarlet idol, big or little as chance may choose, but always disgustingly ugly — a headless, limbless, formless

'AN ANCIENT AND HONOUR-

MARUTI, THE MONKEY GOD.
(A Nepalese edition of him.)

mass, with a distant approach to the design of a sitting figure, always daubed with scarlet and regarded with reverent awe. He is an ancient and honourable member of the Hindu pantheon,[1] and rules vast territories. Over 1,000 miles away in Nepal, among the Himalayas, comparatively artistic images of him sit under sacred umbrellas and receive adoration.

[1] 'Hanuman or Maruti, a black-faced monkey with his tail conspicuously flourishing round his head, is the special guardian of Mahratta villages. Around the temple of Rama particularly, crowds of monkeys gather and are held to be sacred.
'Wealth and labour could not have been devoted to baser practices than in the erection of the vast enclosures dedicated to Siva and Vishnu. Even the sacred monkeys . . . are disgraced by association with indescribable vileness.'

On the side walls of Maruti's kennels are two little shelf projections, like tiny basins put to catch the drip of a tap at home. In the left of these flowers are offered, and on the right water is poured. Dirty stream-marks down the wall and puddles on the earth floor add to the offensive appearance of the shrine. Little stone adornments may cap the hutch, and in the larger buildings a bell hangs in the doorway, rung by worshippers to draw the attention of the idol. There, too, the everywhere prevailing stone bull is to be found, lying in front of the idol seat, looking towards it with an air of solemn, passive wonder.

Dozens and scores of people, mostly men and boys (for very few women are anywhere to be seen) gather around us whenever I stop the *gari* and get down with my guide to see what Hindu temples actually are. Sometimes the shrine is very sacred, no European being allowed within. The larger temples—Vishnu's, Gunputti's, Siva's—have little shrines around them, handsome pillared entrances, shaven priests, and the perpetual bull gazing unconsciously towards the central idol.

Worshippers pour water over the stone bull's back.

'Why do they do that?' I ask.

'Worship,' is the answer.

'What use is it when he can't feel?'

'It is the system.'

This is the constant reply to every query as to underlying reasons. Always the same thing over again.

'Why do you have a stone bull here?'

'It is written in the Puranas.'

'Why do they ring the bell?'

'It is a kind of sign of worshipping the god.'

'Can the god hear the bell?'

'I cannot answer that question.'

'But do you think that he can hear?'

'I would rather not say.'

You turn to another,—'Do *you* think he can hear?'

'No.'

'Then why do you ring the bell?'

'It is the system.'

'It is written in the Vedas, "*Ring the bell*,"!' explains my guide. He is himself a scholar, teaches Marathi in the mission-house, and sees the folly of idolatry, and yet goes on all the same —'It is the system.'

One wayside temple is very pretty: green trees outside, a verandah over the lofty entrance, and a young fellow in red and green and purple looking down; a quiet spot, with little birds flitting past, and a large tree in leaf in the courtyard. The tinkle of the soft bell shows the whereabouts of the idol. A group of men round the door are excitedly discussing the marriage question. Near the priest's house on the courtyard a cow is tethered to the tree. Women, with the usual pretty figures, pass here and there; and children, bright, wee creatures, with jewelled nose-rings, are playing about. They seem to do so freely all over the place, while no European is allowed within the sacred precincts. The latter are dark and gloomy, wooden pillars supporting the low roof, fresco pictures on the wall representing grotesque gods variously occupied. Glass candle-bowls hang from the ceiling, and a decorated canopy stretches over the idol.

'What is this building at the side?' I ask.

'Places for holy men—poor men.' (Pilgrims and fakirs.)

'Do people worship here much?'

'Every day; once a week the chief day.'

'How do they worship?'

'With flowers and water.'

'Can the idols see the flowers or the water?'

'No.'

'Then why?'—etc.

'Have you read the New Testament?' I ask an intelligent-looking young priest.

'Being a Hindu,' he answers, 'I don't wish to read *that*.'

What does he read?
Do you know what he reads—the histories of his idols? Do you know that, as a Bengali newspaper[1] confesses, 'abomination worship is the main ingredient of modern Hinduism'?
Standing in the sunshine and looking into the gloom of the idol hall, the contrast between the Light of the world and India's moral darkness fills the heart. Face to face with CHRIST think of the ideals before us, of SIVA—

KALI.

'Siva, the destroyer, covered with the ashes of funeral fires, drawing a veil over the sun, and driving creation into chaos. A glance from the third eye in his forehead strikes dead those who offend him. His necklace is of human skulls, and his rosary is of the same; serpents writhe in his hair and wreathe his neck.'

Think of these ideals! of KALI—

Kali, wife of Siva, 'an abominable personification of hatred and cruelty.' 'It is scarcely possible to conceive anything more hideous than the images of this goddess. Her body and four arms are dark blue, the hands red, to intimate her delight in blood. . . . The mouth is open wide and the tongue, all red with blood, is hanging out. . . . The hands on the left side are extended in welcome to her worshippers. Those on the right hold a weapon of war and the head of a giant.'

'At her best,' writes Bishop Thoburn, ' Kali is a wretched deity, and no one who comprehends even faintly the blighting effect upon the heart and mind which the adoration of such an object must cause, can think with indifference of the manner in which millions prostrate themselves before this revolting object.'[*]

Siva and Kali are worshipped by myriads.

Krishna is another of Hinduism's ideals,

THE GODDESS KALI.

[1] *The Reis and Rayet*, in an editorial. See *Dawn in India*, the Christian Literature Society's Magazine, July, 1895.

KRISHNA—'The most popular god of India,' over the narrative of whose shameless and abandoned life 'the Pundits allegorise and the common people gloat.'

He is represented by more frequent images than those of any other god. One of the best known is the shapeless hideous idol in Orissa—nothing but a black stump with a head upon it. The difference between it and other images of Krishna is accounted for by the saying that 'his limbs had dropped off on account of his immorality.'

'When I was remonstrating with some Hindus,' writes Dr. Robson, ' on their worshipping a being guilty of such acts as Krishna, they replied very warmly, "Why, these were but his sports. You English have your sports. You have the railway and the steamboat and the telegraph, and no one blames you. Why should you blame Krishna for sporting in *his* way?"'

Naturally 'his way' is followed by his devotees. 'Starting from the worship of a sensual god, they have sunk to his level. . . . The Nemesis of their origin seems to have followed them all.' Consecrating body and soul to the god, supposed to be incarnate in his priests, 'the worshippers throng into the temples . . . and in more esoteric worship emulate the example of their prototype Krishna. . . . But "it is a shame even to speak of those things which are done of them"—in worship.'

'Religious festivals,' writes Mr. Marrat, 'are associated with unspeakable vileness; processions, garlands, instrumental music and wild songs are connected with a moral degradation appalling to contemplate. . . . The corruptions with which Hinduism reeks are such that if the instincts of the people were not better than their creed, India would surpass in crime and vice the worst ages of imperial Rome, and be notorious through the world as one vast sewer overflowing with poisonous pollutions.'

Hinduism is the same to-day as when Macaulay wrote of India:—

'In no part of the world has a religion ever existed more unfavourable to the moral and intellectual health of our race. The Brahmanical mythology is so absurd that it necessarily

ONE OF THE SHRINES OF POONA.
(*From a photograph.*)

debases every mind which receives it as as truth. And with this absurd mythology is bound up an absurd system of physics, an absurd geography, an absurd astronomy. . . .

'All is hideous and grotesque and ignoble. As this superstition is of all superstitions the most irrational and of all superstitions the most inelegant, so is it of all superstitions the most immoral. Emblems of vice are objects of public worship. Acts of vice are acts of public worship. . . .

'Crimes against life, crimes against property, are not only permitted but enjoined by this odious theology. But for our interference human victims would still be offered to the Ganges, and the widow would still be laid on the pile by the corpse of her husband, and be burned alive by her own children.'

We turn away from the dilapidated picturesque old temple —home of what thought, of what iniquity—thinking with amazement that the Church of Jesus Christ still allows this Hindu system to outrage with its secret cult and open festivals the great name of Religion. As Carey said a century ago of those who might be witnesses for Christ, in face of facts like these, 'Staying at home is become sinful in many cases, and will become so more and more.'[8]

Sadly we wend our way out of the 'sacred' precincts among broken old stone fragments of Maroti, Gunputti and the sacred bull, lying about on the ground. In spite of being castaways they are venerated, and the people protest a little when I venture to examine them. Children crowd around us—a sudden swarm of gay mites gathered in half a minute and chased away by a vigorous old wife.

We leave the Hindu holy rooms, garnished with their small what-nots with little brass things stuck on them and gods in gay attire, to visit one last temple, that of the Jains, who seem to a casual glance to combine Hinduism and Buddhism. It is handsomer than any Hindu shrine we have seen to-day. The central building is composed of fine wood-carving, a hundred years old — quite a beautiful structure. Whatever idol lives here they will not let us see. The priest, a quiet, thoughtful man, seems to have never heard of Christianity.

'Do you know *nothing* about Jesus?' I ask him and the others with him—three tall, grave men.

'We have not heard of Him.'

'Have you never seen the Bible?'

'No.'

Solemn, impenetrable faces! Unknown, unreached hearts beating beneath this calm exterior! I try to tell them something through the guide by interpretation, but he hurries me away.

'They do not like us here,' he explains. 'They do not like me—a Brahmin. *I* cannot tell them Christianity!'

Chapter VIII

RAMABAI

RAMABAI.

'The Chinese have a deity Kwan Yin—goddess of mercy—once a woman of such courage and devotion that she merited heaven, and was in the act of entering it, but bethought herself that it would be better to stay outside heaven and help others to reach it, which thereupon she did.'

'ONE SUNNY INDIAN MORNING, half a century ago, before the first zenana had been opened to missionary work, a Hindu father, bathing in the sacred river Godavery, noticed a fine-looking man coming down to bathe. After the ablutions and the morning prayers were over the father inquired of the stranger who he was, and on learning his caste, clan, dwelling place, and that he was a widower, offered him his little daughter, only nine years old, in marriage. Matters were settled within an hour, the marriage took place next day, and the little girl passed into the possession of the stranger, who took her nearly nine hundred miles away from her home.

'The parents, who were on a religious pilgrimage, left the Godavery next morning with the light hearts of Hindus who have managed to marry their daughter into a prosperous family.

'Fortunately the child bride had fallen into good hands. Her husband, a Brahman Pundit, was a man of Europeanized views

HELPING OTHERS TO REACH HEAVEN

about the education of women. Married as a boy of ten to a little girl, he had given up his project that she should be taught to read when the elders of the family demurred; but when he came to manhood and his wife died, he resolved that if ever he married again he would have his own way in the matter; and now as a widower he carried his new little bride away and immediately began to teach her Sanscrit. Mother-in-law and elders objecting as before, he left home, journeyed to a remote forest among the Western Ghauts, and took up his abode in the jungle. The first night was spent without shelter of any kind. A tiger across the ravine made the darkness hideous with its cries; the little bride, wrapped tightly in her *pasodi* (cotton quilt), lay on the ground convulsed with terror, while the husband kept watch till daybreak, when the hungry beast disappeared. The wild animals of the jungle were around them, and hourly terrified the lonely little girl, but the lessons went on without hindrance. A rude dwelling was constructed, and after a few years little children came to the home in the forest,' among them one whose name has since become a household word to thousands—a bright synonym for Indian Christian work for India's women—RAMABAI.

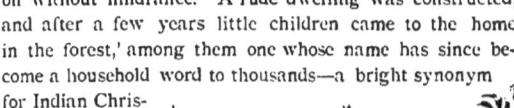

Here at Poona and at Christmas a welcome message comes — 'On Sunday afternoon Ramabai wants you to come and speak to her widows.'

'THROUGH STREETS LIT BY A BLAZING GLARE OF CHRISTMAS SUNLIGHT.'

A drive in a bullock-bandy through streets lit by a blazing glare of Christmas sunlight, a few moments waiting in a pleasantly furnished parlour, the hot afternoon air fanning in from the verandah through open doors and windows, and then an Indian lady enters and greets us cordially. She is middle-aged and slightly deaf, with black hair, an olive-coloured skin, and clear blue eyes. An atmosphere of quiet power surrounds her. You watch this little woman in her white widow's dress—the native dress of plain material loosely wound and pleated without any of the dressmaking to which we are accustomed; you watch her as she sits in the next room presently among her girls, with her dark hair cut short and loosely hanging, and her bare feet slipped out of her shoes in Eastern fashion; you notice the bright intelligence with which she listens, you recall the story of her brave and noble life, and you feel an interest in her and her girls that is not easy to express.

Thirty or forty of them are here, Ramabai's widows, young things, sweet-looking many of them, in their loose flowing wrappers, with dark attentive eyes fixed on the speaker. You think of what they represent—India's women, India's child-widows. A dim, unexplored realm of

A YOUNG INDIAN WIDOW.
(From a photograph taken on entering Ramabai's home.)

suffering and degradation opens at the name. One hundred and forty-five million women, multitudes of whom never go beyond the four walls of their house; many who are wives, and sometimes mothers, before they reach their teens; millions who, though never wives in anything but name, live through the life-long misery of Hindu widowhood. You think of these as you look at the quiet faces of the girls before you, and you thank God for the free and noble ideal of Christian womanhood which He has given Ramabai, and which by prayer and effort she is helping to make real.

It was a strange providence that led her to this place.

Half a lifetime has passed away since the little jungle baby, whose parents had paid such a cost for woman's culture, first saw light.

Among her earliest memories she recalls her mother's lessons 'when the little maiden, heavy with sleep, was tenderly lifted from her bed upon the earth, and wakened with many endearments and sweet mother words, to learn, while the birds about them in the forest chirped their morning songs, lessons from no other book than the mother's lips.'

From that jungle to the pleasant home at Poona is a far cry. Through days of pilgrimage and study with her parents, when 'refusing,' as she says, 'to throw me into the well of ignorance by giving me in marriage in my infancy,' they developed her rare talent till under their instruction she became a 'prodigy of erudition'; through pilgrimages with them and her brother, till in the crisis of an Indian famine the father and mother died, and the orphans, too poor to pay for other help, were obliged themselves to carry the burden of their remains to the place of burning; through long journeys over the continent of India, in which, as penniless pilgrims, she and her brother advocated female education in the Punjab, Rajputana, the Central Provinces, Assam, Bengal, and Madras; through days of popularity at Calcutta, when the young Sanscrit scholar and lecturer created a sensation by her advanced views and scholarship, winning the title of Pundita, never before bestowed upon a woman; through months of loneliness after her brother's death, through a brief, happy marriage that lasted not two years, her husband, a Calcutta graduate, dying of cholera; through motherhood and widowhood, and through missionary journeys to England and the States, Ramabai was led into the Christlike work which has made her name beloved by all who care for India's women in England, America, and her own land.

'I felt a restless desire to go to England,' she writes. 'I could not have done this unless my faith in God had become strong; it is such a great step for a Hindu woman to cross the sea. One shuts oneself for ever off from one's own people. But the Voice came to me as to Abraham . . . and I went forth not knowing whither I went.'

She returned to give her life to the service of India's women. To rescue and uplift suffering widows, she founded her Poona home.

A GROUP OF RAMABAI'S WIDOWS, IN TRAINING.

'Help me,' she writes, 'to educate the high-caste child-widows, for I solemnly believe that this hated and despised class of women, educated and enlightened, are, by God's grace, to redeem India!'

Eight years have passed since Ramabai's Home was opened. Many girls have left it for useful Christian lives.

Some are happy wives of educated men; four are in hospitals, training as nurses; ten are engaged in educational work; and others devoting their time to rescuing their tempted and fallen sisters.

It is a homelike household, big

girls going on to the matriculation standard, and little ones still in kindergarten.

From a neutral position as regards Christianity, Ramabai's school has become distinctly Christian. The baptism of some of the pupils has alienated the non-Christian supporters of the work, and it needs support, having lately with Christ-like love and large-heartedness opened its doors to receive 300 famine orphans.

'Some months ago,' writes Ramabai,[1] 'I heard of the distress of the people in Central India, and at once my heart went out to them in sympathy. Common sense said, "You had better stop here. You have no means, and no strength to do what you wish. You will not be held responsible for not helping those famine people. Indeed, what can a weak woman do? Besides, the Government of India and other benevolent people are doing what they can. There is nothing for you to do."

'I tried to quiet my conscience in this manner, but louder and louder spoke the voice of God within my heart till I could no longer keep still.

'I went; and ever since I have seen the girls of the famine districts —some fallen into the hands of wicked people; some ruined for life and turned out by their cruel masters owing to bad diseases, to die a miserable death; some being treated in the hospitals, only to be taken back into the pits of sin, there to await a cruel death; some bearing the burdens of sin, utterly lost to the sense of shame and humanity—hell has become a horrible reality to me, and my heart is bleeding for those daughters of fond parents who have died leaving them orphans. Who with a mother's heart and a sister's love can rest without doing everything in her power to save at least a few of the girls who can yet be saved from the hands of the evil ones? So, regardless of the

FAMINE VICTIMS IN THE CENTRAL PROVINCES.
(*From a photograph.*)

[1] *Famine Experiences*, by Pundita Ramabai.

trying financial state of my school, I went to work in the Central Provinces to get a few of the helpless young widows.'

Over 140 girls were rescued through this effort, and as soon as they were housed and cared for Ramabai set to work again.

'The Lord,' she writes, 'put it into my mind to save three hundred girls out of the famine districts. The funds sent to me by my friends in America are barely enough to feed and educate fifty girls, and people ask how I am going to support all these others.

'I do not know, but the Lord knows what I need. I can say with the Psalmist, "I am poor and needy, yet the Lord thinketh upon me," and He has promised that "Ye shall eat in plenty and be satisfied, and praise the name of the Lord your God that hath dealt wondrously with you: and My people shall never be ashamed." My girls and I are quite ready to forego all our comforts, give up luxuries and live as plainly as we can. We shall be quite contented to have only one meal of common coarse food daily if necessary, and so long as we have a little room or a seer of grain left in this house, we shall try and help our sisters who are starving.

THE SHARADA SADAN, RAMABAI'S HOME AT POONA.

'Want of means to support the girls was not the only difficulty I had to face on my return home from the Central Provinces. The plague had come on us. The suburban municipality of Poona came down upon me like a thunder-storm. I was to remove over one hundred girls within two days.

'I had put up sheds for them in the compound, but the sheds were of no use now. . . . I had to send the girls twenty miles away. They had no proper shelter. The water was bad and sun very hot. A nice healthy child died of sunstroke a week after the removal, several became very ill, and two died later on. They were too weak to stand hardships. Removal increased sickness, expense, and anxiety, but I was upheld by the merciful Father.

'We have a large piece of ground at Kedgaum, about forty miles from here, but there are no shade trees near, and to live there in the hot season is not safe.

'THE LITTLE ONE' 91

SOONDERBAI POWAR
AND RAMABAI.

But there was no other place where I could take my girls. So several large sheds were erected. I took all my girls there. The heat was intense. They got fever and sore eyes. Our old girls and some of the helpers are suffering. . . . My eyes have been nearly blinded, and I cannot do much writing, and my business has to be neglected against my wish. *A house must be built to shelter the girls.* . . .

'In the meantime the wild famine girls are divided into little classes and given in charge of their trained sisters. They are learning regular habits and getting to be quite nice and civilised. Each girl has some work to do, and learns in school certain hours of the day. My old girls have nobly come forward to assist.

'It is quite pleasing to see them vieing with each other in doing deeds of kindness and helping their new sisters. The youngest girl in charge of one of the classes is only fourteen, but has twenty-three small children in her charge, besides a famine baby which she has adopted. One of our babies was found by a policeman on the roadside. No one knows whose she is nor what her name is. The child seemed to have lost all sense. She would neither cry nor laugh nor smile, and would sit for hours like a stone statue, her sad little head turned on one side. She would not talk nor ask for food, if no one gave her anything to eat, nor would she cry for hunger and pain, if beaten by unkind famine girls. This was most sad to see, and I could not bear to leave the little one and come away.'

And can we bear to leave them?

No work in India deserves our help and sympathy more than this Poona Home. A recent mail has brought me a letter from Soonderbai Powar, Ramabai's faithful helper, containing news of the baptism of over 200 girls, many of them famine orphans.

'Is this not good news,' writes Soonderbai, ' for you and for all God's children? We shall really have a happy New Year. We are praising the Lord and rejoicing in Him, safe under His mighty wings.'

Chapter IX
A LODGE IN THE WILDERNESS

A herculean task lies still before them. . . . Yet the extent of territory gained in Eastern countries by the champions of the Cross in the past century is greater than that in any other century in the history of Eastern Missions. They have not forgotten that more than three centuries were needed for the conversion of the Roman Empire in Europe, and so they battle on in quiet confidence, being persuaded that the weapons of their warfare are mighty, through GOD, to the ultimate victory of Christian truth, and the final extension of Christ's Kingdom to the uttermost ends of the earth.—SIR MONIER WILLIAMS, K.C.E.I.

SIX o'clock in the morning.

Wide bars of radiant moonlight, broken by black shadows, fall on the dim mosquito curtains of the bed. In the open window square of dim grey sky, stars apparently indicate midnight. Ten minutes later you open your eyes again. Daylight is streaming in, and to catch the flying beauty of the tropic dawn you fling Indian muslins round you and steal out through the open dressing-room door into the cool compound, where nothing and no one else ever comes at this hour, to enjoy twenty minutes of brief sweet freshness before the sun sends you indoors. Just before sunrise is the loveliest time of day, only equalled by the evening and the moonlight, when the dark verandah or the silence of the flat roof bewitch you into hours of dreamy rest and wonder at the beauty of sky and stars.

'MID-INDIA LIES AROUND—HUGE, HOT, SANDY.'

How far we are from Poona now, and how far off from home! Winter away in England—frost on trees and hedgerows, while with us a blazing tropic sun pours down on the bare, brown, naked earth. Not a blade of grass to be seen, scarcely a tree.

Mid-India lies around us, a far-stretching wilderness reached from the west by a long railway run across the Deccan, a huge hot sandy waste sprinkled with scanty towns, bushes, plantains and toddy trees. The strangest rocks are scattered on the plain, now looking like ruined castles, now like glacier moraines. Burnt yellow, red or greyish, rounded by millenniums of weather wear, massed in jagged hills or flung wide over the country, they reach for hundreds of miles, and the train winds among them like a serpent creeping across a desert. After the Mutiny people were afraid, and the line was laid avoiding large population centres—a plan now regretted, I believe.

You feel yourself in an empty world. Sometimes a faint smoke shows hidden huts, perhaps a distant village, possibly a town, but it does not look possible. Sometimes you cross a river, a dried-up immense channel with a long massive bridge, and a few pitiful rivulets creeping among parched stones. In the rainy season there will be water here, which will very likely sweep the bridge away. Now mere streamlets half lost in burning sand! Magic dawns and sunsets paint the sky. You travel on, and on, and on, sleeping, eating, sleeping again, all night, all day, until the second night you reach this wayside station, Anantapur, a little cluster of native homes surrounded by flat sand wastes. Near the town stands the London Mission House, a pleasant bungalow with half a dozen rooms, and a compound containing stables, servants' quarters, and native Christians' homes.

The workers here, Mr. and Mrs. Hinkley and Miss Christlieb, itinerate their great parish of 700 villages by rail, bicycle, and pony. Come with us in fancy down to the bazaar and see the kind of work they do. Inside the bullock bandy we are sheltered from the blazing sun, but—this furnace blast of a January breeze! What it must be in summer! The little town is crowded with black figures in gay gowns. Twisting the tails of the much-enduring bullocks, the bandy driver wedges through to the market square, stops at a wayside tree, and we dismount.

MRS. HINKLEY.

Oh, the feeling of it, after years of writing and speaking and thinking about the heathen, to stand for the first time in an utterly heathen city, where no mission work is done by any but those with whom you are, a heathen town of six or seven thousand people, with idols, temples, mosques and shrines, but no meeting-house or church—to stand there hemmed in by a crowd of actual living heathen! The droning native hymns swell up accompanied by a sort of East Lon-

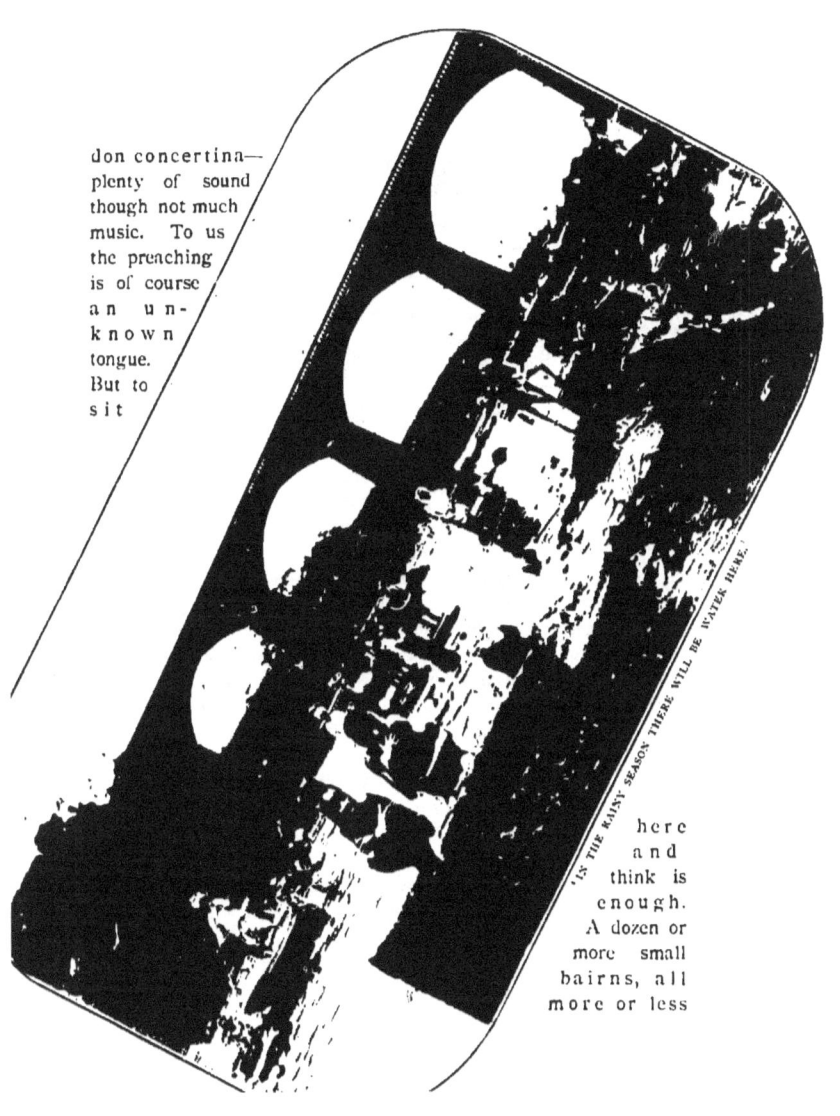

don concertina—
plenty of sound
though not much
music. To us
the preaching
is of course
an un-
known
tongue.
But to
sit

IN THE RAINY SEASON THERE WILL BE WATER HERE.

here
and
think is
enough.
A dozen or
more small
bairns, all
more or less

'WHEN HE SAW THE MULTITUDES HE

naked (rather more than less), stand in front—the oddest little creatures, shy, curious, and afraid, actually afraid of being smiled at! The European child is pleased when you smile at it, and smiles cheerfully back again, but here you smile down at the little ones, and they look gravely at you, push backwards and vanish in the press! At first you think the child was going any way; but smiling at another, you find the same result. The sense of being singled out for the white *Mem Sahib's* observation seems to strike terror to the little hearts, and they swiftly shrink into the crowd. Plenty of others come forward, however,—thin, brown, large-eyed children, like the men, with, as Kipling puts it,—

'Nothing much in front,
And rather less than 'alf of that behind.'

But one gets accustomed to bare brown skin, and only wonders at the hairiness and thinness of the Hindu human being. One shockingly thin old gentleman listens with such interest, his eyes fixed on the speaker, his head rocking from side to side to emphasise the points. All listened attentively, tall men with intelligent faces, some strong, others worn and weary. One handsome-looking fellow on some high ground opposite, with a mocking, clever, careless face, like Mephistopheles, interrupts the speaker by light questions. People shift to and fro, some going, others filling up the spaces. A few women with brown naked babies astride upon their hips creep in and listen with dark uplifted eyes. And as one looks one realises the kind of Eastern crowds that must have gathered long ago around the LORD; realises too, though dimly, how what we feel He must have felt, intensified by His infinitude of knowledge—the inward world of consciousness of GOD, of His love and purposes and glory, a world so utterly unknown to these, a world so difficult to make them know!

This simple Gospel preaching is not without effect. Though it is only a little while since our friends left Bellary to open this out station, and though their parish is so large that it takes them a full year to get half round it, whole villages already wish to become Christian. Persecution springs up to shake the would-be converts—*e.g.*, the following story, in progress as I write:

'In one of our out-stations,' writes Mr. Hinkley, 'the caste people utterly destroyed our school, and went on to prevent our people purchasing a single article in the village. We opened a shop of our own, making the teacher salesman, and built a second school after great difficulty. The work seemed progressing a little till the question arose in the inventive Hindu mind, "If the school be burned down, will he not go away?"

'Within

THE L.M.S. MISSION HOUSE AT BELLARY.

'BUILDED TOGETHER FOR AN HABI-

three days it was done, and the forty families who had sent their children or attended school themselves were driven from their employ and became for the time dependent upon us.

'As soon as possible I got possession of a piece of waste land—alas! hard and barren as a rock for want of rain. We sank two wells, got a little water, and raised a very small crop; but in consequence of hindrances set up at every juncture by village authorities and almost every grade of native official, we are still in doubt whether the land will be granted to us or not.

'In the meantime the persons who destroyed the school set upon, wounded, and beat the teacher; and, following a common custom among Hindus, sad to say too often successful in a land where false witness counts just as much as true, brought a double charge of drunkenness and assault against their victim before he had time to get medical evidence of his condition and lay the true complaint. The innocent man has been fined and the guilty set free, a result which augurs ill for the future; but our hope is in Him who shall deliver the poor and needy, and rid them out of the hand of the wicked.'

Such are some of the experiences that make missionary life out in this wilderness anything but a holiday task. Thinking of which, and of this great parched oven of a parish with its seven hundred villages, our hearts go out to the other workers, few and far between, who, scattered throughout India, are helping to raise that Unseen Temple which, fashioned out of living stones and silently arising in the midst of an unregarding world, is being 'builded together for an habitation of God.' How few the builders are among India's many millions, the annexed diagram suggests rather than shows.

'The missionaries of Reformed Christendom to the three hundred millions of India have increased fourfold in the last forty years. Yet how miserable small is their number—seventeen hundred—at the opening of the second century of India's evangelisation! But from Buddhist Mandalay on the far north-east, where Britain marches

COMPARATIVE POPULATIONS.

GERMAN EMPIRE
49¾ MILLION PERSONS

AUSTRIA HUNGARY
41½ MILLION PERSONS

FRANCE
38¼ MILLION PERSONS

GREAT BRITAIN AND IRELAND
37 MILLION PERSONS

ITALY
30¾ MILLION PERSONS

SPAIN
17⅞ MILLION PERSONS

OTHER PARTS OF EUROPE
43⅞ MILLION PERSONS

INDIA
287 MILLION PERSONS
A larger number than all the above countries combined

'INDIA'S MANY MILLIONS.'

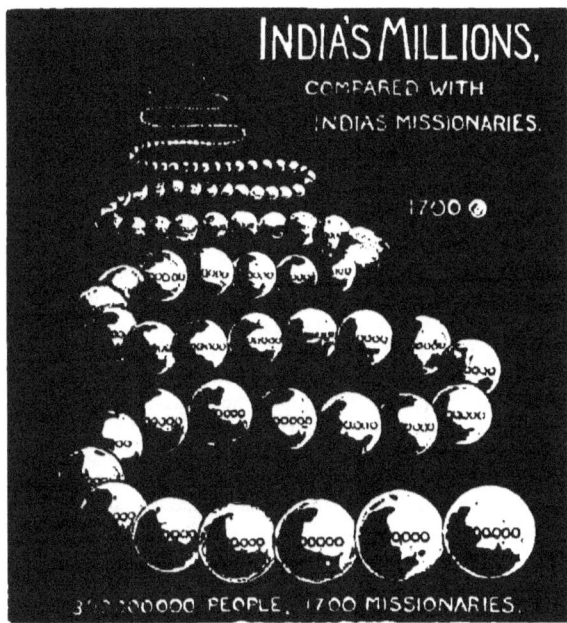

with China, right west for two thousand miles to Mohammedan Quetta between Afghanistan and Persia, and from that lofty base-line down on either side of the great Hindu Peninsula to Cape Comorin, the land has been for the first time taken possession of for Jesus Christ, and only the little faith of every Christian delays the coming conversion of India.

'There is now no great native State in India, Hindu or Mohammedan, in which there are not Christian missionaries and churches. There only, in all the world of Islam, are Mohammedans constrained to be tolerant.

'The supernatural power of Christianity and the secondary influences of Western science and literature have now been allowed for the first time in the history of Asia fairly to take their place side by side with all the agencies of the Hindu, the Mohammedan and the aboriginal religious and social systems. The result is a revolution, silent, subtle and far-reaching, which works in each successive generation with increasing force.

'From the day which put Christianity, though the avowed faith of the ruling race, on the same equal platform as Hinduism, Parseeism, Buddhism, Mohammedanism, Animism, and all other purely human modes of propitiating God, as Christ Himself put it before His Roman judge, the conversion of India to the one true and living God became an assured certainty.'⁹

Already we can see the building rising. Amid difficulty and hindrance, it is day by day extending, breaking down ancient obstructions of caste and idolatry, lifting its living stones into the light and air. It is not yet 100 years since the first convert of the nineteenth century was baptized by William Carey in the waters of the Ganges, but to-day among the religions of India Christianity holds a place.

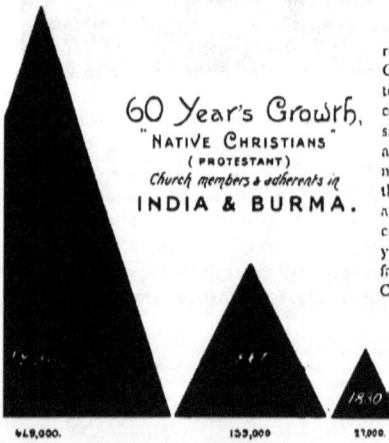

60 Year's Growth, "NATIVE CHRISTIANS" (PROTESTANT) Church members & adherents in INDIA & BURMA.

[The three black pyramids represent the growth of the Church in India from 1830 to 1890, including not only communicants, but thousands of baptized persons of all ages, and also the broad margin of adherents, who, though we cannot hope they are all by any means really converted men and women, yet have left their heathen faiths and become professing Christians.]

'We who began our Indian career in 1853,' writes Dr. George Smith, 'who witnessed the Mutiny in 1857, took part in the reorganisation of the administration in 1858-1861, and rejoiced in the increase at that time of missionary efforts, would have pronounced it incredible that, ten years before the end of the nineteenth century, there would be more Christians than Sikhs in India, and that the rate of increase of native Christians in the martial races of the Punjab, Mohammedan and Hindu, would be six hundred per cent. every decade.'

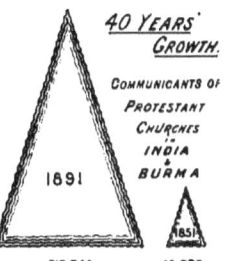

40 YEARS' GROWTH.
COMMUNICANTS OF PROTESTANT CHURCHES INDIA & BURMA
1891 — 215,759.
1851 — 15,000.
[The two grey pyramids represent communicants only.]

As morning by morning the group of about a dozen native Christians, fathers and mothers and dear wee bairns, gather to prayers in the little dining-room of this simple mission house—as they sit there, squatting on the uncarpeted floor, with bare feet, scanty garments, and attentive, reverent faces, listening to the reading and exposition, given in what is to us an unknown tongue—as they sing their 'songs of Zion,' set to plaintive Indian airs—we think of the great company to which they belong, and which, gathered from east and west and north and south of India, shall yet join the chorus of the celestial city and 'sit down with Abraham and Isaac and Jacob in the kingdom of heaven.'

It is a dream, you say? It is not coming? Is this forty years' increase of native ministers a dream? Is the last twenty years' increase of the native Church in India, both of her leaders as well as of her rank and file, a dream? Yes, thank God, it is a dream—one of His dreams, a thing too beautiful and wonderful and lasting to be anything but real.

40 Years' Increase
OF THE
NATIVE ORDAINED MINISTRY
IN INDIA, 1851–1890.

[In 1851 there were twenty-five native ordained ministers in India. In 1890 there were seven hundred and ninety-seven—a forty-fold increase in forty years.]

'THE KINGDOM OF GOD COMETH

Twenty Years' Growth

OF THE

Christian Church

1871

1890

WOMEN WORKERS (Foreign and Eurasian), 370.
(Each candle = 200.)

FOREIGN MISSIONARIES, MEN, 438.
(Each candle = 200.)

NATIVE WOMEN WORKERS, 837.
(Each candle = 500.)

NATIVE MEN WORKERS, 2,210.
(Each candle = 500.)

NATIVE PROTESTANT COMMUNICANTS, 52,813.
(Each candle = 10,000.)

'NATIVE CHRISTIANS' (Protestant), 224,161.
(Each candle = 20,000.)

WOMEN WORKERS (Foreign and Eurasian), 711. (Each candle = 200.)

FOREIGN MISSIONARIES, MEN, 986.
(Each candle = 200.)

NATIVE WOMEN WORKERS, 3,278.
(Each candle = 500.)

NATIVE MEN WORKERS, 4,988.
(Each candle = 500.)

NATIVE PROTESTANT COMMUNICANTS, 182,722.
(Each candle = 10,000.)

NATIVE CHRISTIANS' (Protestant adherents), 559,661.
(Each candle = 20,000.)

IN

India.

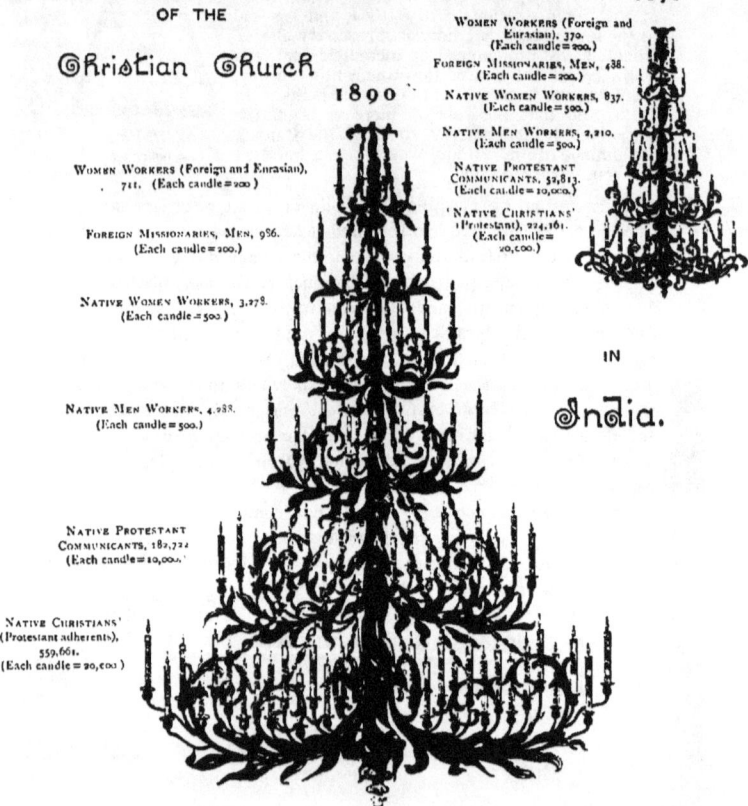

It is His dream, but we only see it dimly—only a little bit of it thus far. What can we gauge of it? Cold, hard figures! Narrow numerical ratios, utterly inadequate to represent spiritual advance. For not in numbers only does the Kingdom come. The hand of Jesus Christ, delivering from sin and fear, lifting hearts into personal holiness, purifying the home, protecting little children, rescuing womanhood from a thousand nameless woes, sanctifying marriage and social relations, bringing love into a selfish world, a heathen world—this mighty unseen Hand produces other than arithmetical results. The influence of a Christian atmosphere, the far-reaching effects of Christian education, the vast transforming influences which come to every country that receives for the first time the Bible and Christian literature,—these things cannot be exhibited diagrammatically. But these things are the things which Christ has brought.

'Do not let us be tempted to make the vulgar, the shallow mistake of estimating the value of a Christian mission by the mere number of the converts that it claims. The presence in a heathen or Muslim district of a man who, filled with the missionary spirit, exhibits in his preaching, and so far as may be in his life, the self-denying and the Christian virtues, who is charged with sympathy for those among whom his lot is cast, who is patient of disappointment and failure, and of the sneers of the ignorant or the irreligious, who works steadily on with a single eye to God's glory and the good of his fellow-men, is of itself an influence for good and a centre from which it radiates, wholly independent of the number of converts he is able to enlist. By the influence of such a man, simply following his Lord and Master, many a Moslem may be truly Christianised, or be entered on any record of missionary successes, but whose name may, nevertheless, well be entered in the book of life. Who will dare—who will wish—to fix a limit to the great muster roll of the past, the present and the future? "Those who are not against Me are on My side." " In every nation he that feareth God and worketh righteousness is accepted of Him "' [10]

Well, we have wandered far from this little mission bungalow, a lodge in the wilderness! Before we leave it altogether shall we let our hearts go out, not to the work achieved, but to that which is still waiting? Among the scattered Christian homes of this great Southern India is that of Thomas Patient, one of our own college men, who has an even larger 'parish' round

MR. PATIENT'S BUNGALOW AT MALVALLI, MYSORE.

him in Mysore than that of the Hinkleys here, and who makes a special plea for a needy section south of his Malvalli centre.

'For about 100 miles,' he writes, 'the Coimbatore district is still unoccupied. Something is done in Kollegal, but from there to Satyamanglam nothing but occasional itinerant work is attempted.

'The Wesleyans have laboured in Mysore for fifty years, but the harvest here is plenteous, and the labourers but few.

'I doubt whether with all our efforts we even keep pace with the growth of the population, not to speak of overtaking the heathendom around. We have in Mysore some 5,000 native Christians (nominal and real), but 94 per cent. are still sunk in superstition and ungodliness. Notwithstanding the good work being done in every district, there remaineth yet much land to be possessed.'

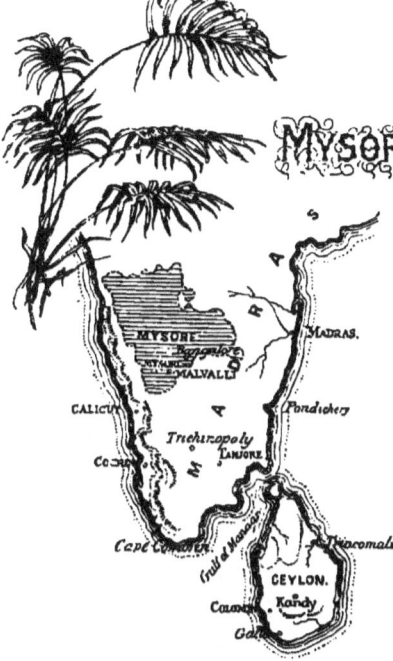

MYSORE.

Look at the map of this beautiful Native State, MYSORE, a country larger than Greece, covering 28,000 square miles, and with 5,500,000 people, as many as all Ireland, scattered in 17,000 villages, hamlets, and towns. Think of this lovely upland plain—between the Eastern and Western Ghauts, which narrowed here in South India, skirt three sides of the State—and try to realise what it means to the Mysore missionaries that their average parish numbers 275,000 souls! They cannot attempt to do any special work for Parsees, Mohammedans or Jains, and no converts have yet been won from these classes in Mysore. To give even one worker even to every county in the State, over fifty more missionaries are wanted. When will these men and women come?

But MYSORE's needs are little, and MYSORE itself small, compared to the vast native State of HYDERABAD, the Nizam's dominions of 82,000 square miles lying north of this little lodge in

◊ = AVERAGE PARISH OF A MINISTER AT HOME—1000 souls.

AVERAGE PARISH OF A HYDERABAD MISSIONARY 433,000 souls.⟶
(Each ◊ = 1000 people.)

HYDERABAD CITY: THE CHIEF STREET, SHOWING THE CHAR MINAR.

SPIRITUAL DESTITUTION OF HYDERABAD

the wilderness. Larger than Portugal and Roumania put together, nearly as large as Turkey in Europe, and with a population of 13,000,000—more than twice that of MYSORE; this immense region has only thirty workers, one on an average to 433,000 souls. Few parts of India are as neglected by the Church as this great Moslem country.[11] In the Telugu-speaking part of the State each man has 500,000 hearts to reach. And this in hot South India, not in a closely peopled country where scores of thousands can be evangelised in cities, but in vast village-covered regions, among hill tribes in mountains, on burning plains, hundreds of miles in length, and through wide 'districts teeming with people.'

Around the Hinkleys' station here lies MADRAS, the great Eastern Presidency, containing sections almost as dark.

In innumerable centres throughout these three populous lands, to-night, as the sun goes down, white-turbaned followers of the False Prophet will gather to minaretted mosques, and untold multitudes will bow before senseless idols, as they bowed in blindness yesterday when we forgot about them, as they will bow to-morrow, and to-morrow, and to-morrow, unless—

Can we again forget?

Chapter X

IN A MOFUSSIL MOSQUE

When Zeid had . . . resolved to divorce her, we joined her in marriage unto thee; lest a crime should be charged on the true believers in marrying the wives of their adopted sons . . . the command of God is to be performed. No crime is to be charged on the prophet, as to what God hath allowed him.

And if ye fear that ye shall not act with equity . . . take in marriage of such other women as please you, two, or three, or four. Ye may with your substance provide wives for yourselves.—(KORAN, chaps. 33 and 34.)

ETHICS OF ISLAM, *Dr. Post (Beirut)*.

'WHAT is this gateway here?'

Passing through the little town we have drawn rein at some light iron gates behind an almost empty tank.

The trusty syce replies in fluent Canarese, affording but small light.

'We may go in, mayn't we?'

My little Arab's confident advance makes the question intelligible, and a grave-looking Moslem inside the white railings, attired in flowing robes, lets us in.

It is evening. Just behind us women coming to draw water are climbing down the rough steps of a pit-like tank. As the high gates swing open, and we pass in at a foot-pace, my little Arab steed might feel on native ground. For this simple enclosure, with its travellers' rest-house, and central building standing out against the sky, its white walls, flat roof, white dome and minarets, is Arabia's gift to India.

'A mosque, syce?'

'*Mem Sahib*, mosque! Mosque.'

Sitting here in the saddle, while the horse stands quietly, as if

ISHMAEL

conscious of some sacred influence, we watch the groups of turbaned men gathering about the open *façade* of the mosque. Silently they observe us, commenting in undertones—an Englishwoman on horseback has probably never been inside these gates before. The headman, perhaps a *moulvie*, comes up and salutes us with a few courteous but incomprehensible words.

An old man with an air of peculiar intentness about him now arrives, and climbing a little eminence, rings out a clear far-reaching cry—the Moslem call to prayer. Once—again—again—again, he sends across the town and out into the wide and bare surrounding country that summons which is echoing in this twilight from the lips of thousands of such *muezzins*, at thousands of such mosques throughout Moslem India.

A hush falls on the gathering. The curious glances which greeted us are exchanged for a look towards Mecca; and leaving their shoes at the entrance, the men pass gravely into the mosque to pray.

Silently we wait. The *muezzin* descends and follows. The ground is almost empty. Behind the white-domed roof a tropic sunset is illuminating the sky. Exquisite changing colours—gold, saffron, crimson, rose—shoot up into the overhanging purples and sapphire grey. The mosque stands silhouetted against a sea of flame. As every moment passes the living west burns brighter. These dull white walls and silent minarets, this rounded dome clear cut upon the flashing glories of a mid-India sunset, stamp themselves on the brain.

Pausing by the little

'DOWN THE VILLAGE STREET.'

'ONE OF THE GREATEST AN-

'FROM DISTANT NORTH AFRICA.'

rest-house, for a few quiet minutes before we turn away, shall we gather up the meaning of this scene to carry with us?

In the market square, down the village street, an idol car is standing. There is no idol here. Hindu temples full of gods, great and small, stand out along the highways by which we have just come. There is nothing here but an empty shrine — a place of prayer to the Unseen. And a sense almost of kinship comes over us, face to face with this younger brother of Judaism — monotheistic Islam, the creed of the 200 millions of the Moslem world, reaching from the Pillars of Hercules to Pekin, from distant North Africa out to the Far East. Yet we are here face to face with what is, alas! no helper, no brother in the faith, but one of the greatest antagonists of Christianity.

For Islam, though it 'represents a spirit of reform working

under the inspiration of a great truth—the truth of the Unity and supremacy of God —and offers immediate access to Him without priest or mediator, leaves a liberal margin for human frailty and passions, and lays no violent hands upon sins of the flesh.' Containing much truth borrowed from Judaism and Christianity, it 'lacks the essentials of saving religion. The modicum of truth is lost in the maximum of error. A counterfeit coin with some grains of pure metal is none the less a deception. One truth mixed with twenty errors will not make a resultant of truth, especially if the twenty errors are in direct opposition to other truths as essential as the one included.'

ONE OF THE MILLIONS OF THE MOSLEM WORLD.

'The Incarnation, the Divinity of Christ, the Trinity, are all stumbling-blocks to the Moslem, and are looked upon rather in the light of ridiculous enigmas than of spiritual truths. To him the doctrine of the Cross and the whole plan of the Atonement is a needless vagary. Islam stands in an attitude of pronounced opposition to Christianity, and not to Christianity only, but to civilisation and all social, intellectual, and spiritual progress.'

Is this so? Can words like these apply to the faith of 60,000,000 in India alone—a Moslem population more than three times greater than that under the Sultan's rule, to count the Moslem subjects of Queen Victoria only—worshipping in some 7,000 mosques up from the simplicity of this Mofussil shrine to the

Moslems under the rule of QUEEN VICTORIA in India.

Moslems under the SULTAN'S rule.

'SAYING PRAYERS FIVE TIMES A DAY WHEREVER THEY MAY BE.'

dream-like loveliness of the Pearl Mosque inside the Fort of Delhi, and to the vast red sandstone courtyards of the Jami Musjid, the largest mosque of India, with its handsome gateways, white marble domes and minarets, and magnificent proportions dwarfing surrounding Delhi, its solemn *moulvies* and *mullahs* sitting cross-legged on their carpets, discussing religious questions, or haranguing crowds of the faithful drawn from the four winds?

Sixty millions, worshipping no idol, saying prayers five times a day—at the first faint blush of dawn, when the *muezzin*'s call rings out across the continent, '*Prayer is more than sleep—is more than sleep!*' at midday wherever they may be, again between 4 and 5 p.m., then at sunset, and again the last thing before sleep—which of us can look thoughtfully on India without taking them into account?

'Whence have they come?' we ask, and the question carries us back across more than 1,000 years—through eleven centuries' story of invasion, war, and conquest, from the days when in the times of our Saxon Heptarchy the first Moslem hordes swept down from Central Asia on helpless Hindustan, on to the time when Moghul conquest rose to empire, under Akbar in the days of 'good Queen Bess,' holding all Northern India and ravaging

'SOLEMN MOULVIES . . SEATED ON THEIR CARPETS DISCUSSING RELIGIOUS QUESTIONS.'

the south; and on again through centuries of magnificence, cruelty, decadence, and ruin, till at the close of the Mutiny forty years ago 'the world had lived to see a knot of English officers in sword and sash sitting round a table in the old imperial capital to try the lineal descendant of the Great Moghul, sometime King of Delhi, and presently a British pensioner, on the charge of disturbing the public peace of India!'[12]

Such a story! One of the romances of real life, more wonderful and sadder than any fiction—North India overrun by swarms of fighting Moghuls, harrying each other and every one else; exacting immense revenues, amid cruelties, such as the man-hunting of Taglak, 'without precedent in the annals of human wickedness'; then the advent of the terrible Timour or Tamerlane, pouring with his armies down the Himalayan passes, capturing Delhi, feasting and thanking God while the streets were heaped with dead, and vanishing back into Central Asia leaving desolation behind: this phase of A.D. 1400 running on

THE TAJ MAHAL.

into the Akbar apotheosis of the next two centuries, when under Aurungzeeb the empire reached its climax, commemorated to all time by the splendour of its buildings, among them the Pearl Mosque of Shah Jehan, 'the purest and loveliest house of prayer in the world,' and that 'dream in marble' the Taj Mahal, raised to the memory of his lost queen Nur Mahal, 'Light of the

World.' And all the while the fall of Moghul power pending from its own inner corruption and unfitness to be—new emperors succeeding, for instance, as a rule by deposing and imprisoning their fathers, and killing their rival brothers off—till at last through rebellions of viceroys and generals, revolts of the conquered but restless Hindus, and through fresh Moghul invasions, the record of ruin began.

* * * *

The creaking of a bullock-cart passing down the roadway recalls us from our reverie on the long, strange answer to the question whence Islam in India came. The sun has dropped behind the western rim of the great open *maidan*. The red glow, a crescent sweep of colour burning half way to the zenith, is fading slowly, beneath the intense radiance of the evening star. We seem to have been watching the very gates of heaven. Now that the west is paling, the glory of a full moon is flooding all the land—a full moon that is lighting thousands of 'the faithful' on their way to Mecca, where 100,000 pilgrims gather every year. Once in his life every good Moslem is supposed to visit the Kaaba, no matter from how far he has to come. And India sends her millions. For though the Moghul Empire fell, the faith remains, imposed by force upon the conquered people, monotheistic and thus purer than the idolatry it ousted, but 'holding the truth in unrighteousness,' and bearing bitter fruit.

THE TAJ SEEN FROM THE FORT, AGRA.

'As a general rule,' writes Bishop Thoburn, 'the Moslem moral standard is a little lower than that of the Hindus, and the same remark will have to be made with regard to their general reputation for morality.'

How should it be otherwise when their 'moral standard' is that of the Koran, which bears about as much relation to

A MOHAMMEDAN MAP OF THE WORLD.

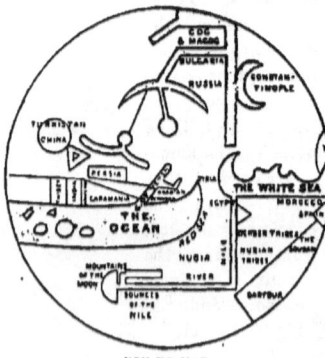

KEY TO MAP.

morality as the Mohammedan maps of the world do to actual continents and seas?

Think, as in the radiant moonlight we turn homeward, while the worshippers, their brief prayers done, go on their way, think of what the homes must be to which they go to-night—homes in which polygamy is only limited by financial considerations. A

MOSLEM PILGRIMS WORSHIPPING AROUND THE KAABA AT MECCA.

"Thousands of the faithful on their way to Mecca, where 100,000 pilgrims gather every year. Once in his life every good Moslem is supposed to visit the Kaaba, no matter from how far he has to come."

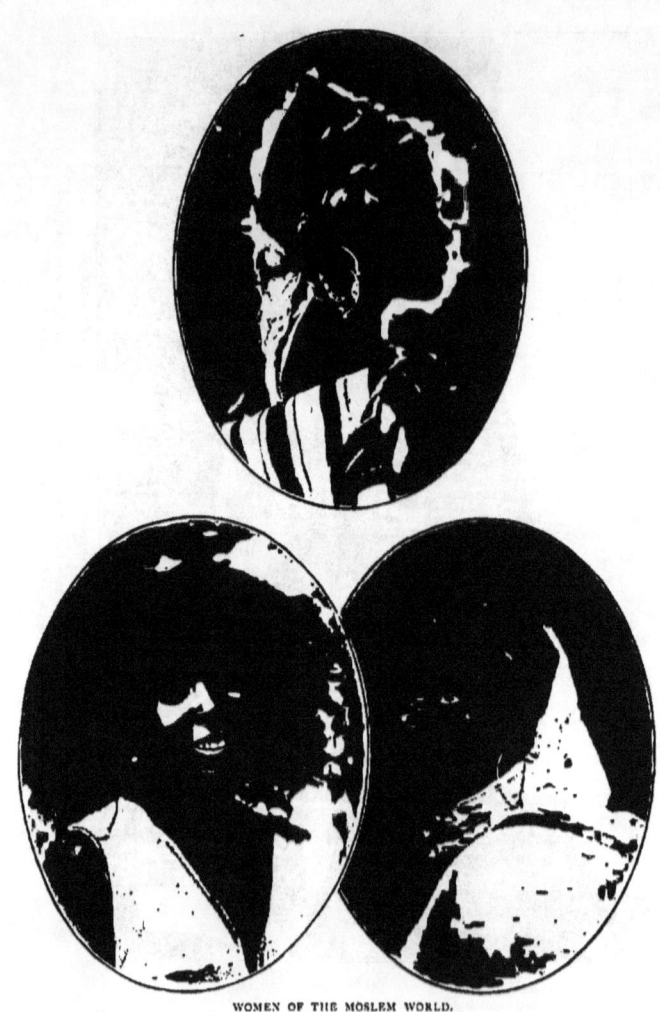

WOMEN OF THE MOSLEM WORLD.

WANTED—INDIAN CHURCH LEADERS

Moslem may have four wives at any one time, and as many slaves—practically wives—as he wants. Any wife is divorced by a word at a moment's notice, divorced without redress, her position being entirely dependent on the chance good temper of her husband.

'O Prophet,' announces a 'special revelation' of the Koran in chapter xxxiii. 'O Prophet, we have allowed thee thy wives, . . . and also the slaves which thy right hand possesseth . . . and the daughters of thy uncles and the daughters of thy aunts . . . who have fled with thee from Mecca, and any other believing woman, if she give herself unto the prophet; in case the prophet desireth to take her to wife.'

Linked to which 'revelation' and in view of India's 60,000,000 Moslems, we recall the words of Bishop Westcott: 'India is the greatest trust ever committed to a Christian nation.'

Is there no meaning in the Providence that has put these 60,000,000 *here* under Christian rule? Is there no meaning in the fact that while 'Moslem converts in any numbers cannot openly be won as yet within the limits of the Turkish Empire, for the Government will not allow the effort to be made, nor is a Moslem's life safe for an hour (except perhaps in Egypt) if he openly becomes a Christian,' here in India even Islam is compelled to learn religious toleration, and her people are free to follow whatever faith they will? Many of the best native Christians have been gathered from Moslem ranks.[13] And this means much for the native Church. For just as India gained from her Mohammedan·conquerors the infusion of a more vigorous element into the national character, the Churches gain by the introduction of these zealous and intense believers.

'They have been,' writes Bishop Thoburn, 'our most unrelenting opponents; but when truly converted the Mohammedan makes not only a devoted Christian, but a superior leader. And leadership is the great want in every mission field.'

Chapter XI
BY THE EASTERN SEA

<blockquote>I should not like it, were you fitted to be a missionary, that you should drivel down into a king.
C. H. SPURGEON.</blockquote>

IT is so hot! I am valiantly trying to write intelligibly, but feel too soft and sticky to hope to accomplish much—a usual condition of feeling at Madras, I should think. It is just noon, and sitting here in a gauze-like dressing gown (after changing twice already), with windows and doors wide open to catch every breath of air, it is strange to think of you at home in the cosy fireside corner, with the poor world cold and white outside, the trees bare, the valley empty—all the dear place with the wintry look that our hearts know so well. If you could see this other place!—could feel the soft warm stillness that falls on everything when the blazing sun is high; could hear the whisper of the pleasant wind in leaves and branches, the distant chatter of the crows, the notes of birds and insects, and see the resplendent sunshine flashing rich

ON THE SHORE, MADRAS.

colour on trees and flowers, and scintillating through the balmy air!

We feel at last in India. Bombay with its crowded city streets, Poona with its dry uplands, and the empty wilderness of Mid-India that we have stayed in for the last three weeks, all came short of one's expectation. But here one is in the India of picture and story—green, fertile, exquisitely coloured, with palms and lakes and creepers, hanging bunches of rich colour out on high tree branches—the India of one's dreams. Irrigation, even in this famine year when all the land elsewhere seems parched for want of water, has made this seaboard overflow with lakes and streams, till it is greener and lovelier than you could guess. If only you could see it! I feel it is impossible with this slow-creeping pen to give you any adequate idea of anything.

This old historic city by the sea, from which Clive sailed to avenge the Black Hole of Calcutta, and to commence that

A MADRAS JUTKA.

series of conquests that won us Northern India, scarcely seems a city. Here, at Royapetta, and for miles around as you drive in the odd wee *jutkas* of the place, with a Jehu *minus* garments, you see little to suggest town life, except the fine Government buildings and the churches here and there. It is more like a congeries of pretty villages, with houses and compounds between—large rambling Eastern houses, flat-roofed, with wide verandahs, half hidden among trees. You might think yourselves miles away from a city, till the whirr and whistle of an electric tram reminds you where you are. Of course there are other quarters—Blacktown, the native section, and crowded business streets; but Madras, with its nine miles sea front, is for the most part of this bowery type. Repose, spaciousness, and the charm of being countrified, counterbalance the long journeys entailed in this 'city of magnificent distances.'

Rich memories centre round Madras, so long the headquarters of that bold and powerful Company, of whose extinction Sir H. S. Maine eloquently wrote :—

'The East India Company—it would be impossible to reflect without emotion on the extinction of so mighty a name. That wonderful succession of events which has brought the youngest civilisation of the world to instruct and correct the oldest, which has reunited those wings of the Indo-European race which separated in the far infancy of time to work out their strangely different missions, which has avenged the miscarriage of the Crusades by placing the foot of the most fervently believing of Christian nations on the neck of the mightiest of Mohammedan dynasties, will inevitably be read by posterity as the work, not of England, but of the English East India Company.'

Here it was that the struggle for supremacy in India was fought out between the French and English in the middle of the eighteenth century, from the day when Madras surrendered to

MOUNTAINS OF TRAVANCORE.

the French squadron almost without a blow, in 1746, the English fugitives hiding for dear life in Fort St. David, on to Clive's daring capture and defence of Arcot, and to Sir Eyre Coote's decisive victories, which fourteen years later 'left not a single ensign of the French nation avowed by the authority of its Government in any part of India.'

And here it is that the greater battle has been, and is being, fought. Of the 44 million people of this Eastern Presidency, over 860,000 are Christians. Far, far back, in the seventh or eighth century, when the old Nestorian Church set out to evangelise the world—the Church which, had it but held the pure Gospel, might have transformed Asia—missionaries reached Madras. Three Persian crosses still stand on St. Thomas' Mount here, one of them on a tablet built into the church wall behind the altar, the

THE OLDEST CHRISTIAN INSCRIPTION IN INDIA—SEVENTH CENTURY.
(From *The Conversion of India*; by kind permission of Dr. George Smith.)

cross in relief on it, and a dove with wings extended—the still familiar sign! Down in Cottayam Church in Travancore a similar tablet, the third and only other witness to this old-time Indian mission, preserves the Syriac inscription:—

'LET ME NOT GLORY EXCEPT IN THE CROSS OF OUR LORD JESUS CHRIST.'

The famous Nestorian tablet of North China dates from the same time, and echoes the same faith. It is beautiful to link that early mission effort with those around us here. The power of the Cross still lives—now indeed one may say for the first time fully lives in India, in the missionary movement of the last two centuries.

Madras City possesses a hundred foreign workers, fifty of whom are men. We have met many of them. Entertained in the most ideal way by Mr. and Mrs. Ward of the London Missionary Society whose hospitality and spiritual helpfulness I cannot attempt to describe, we have seen a dozen sections of the great world Service, from the cathedral-Scotch-kirk with its lofty dome painted to represent the midnight heavens, blue airy spaces and constellations producing a singularly fine effect; and from the magnificent structures of the Bible and Tract Societies with their great lecture halls and extensive business premises, to the fine buildings of the Christian College, the largest missionary educational establishment in the world; and down through the many churches—Episcopal, Presbyterian, Congregational, Methodist, and the rest of the roll—to the various schools (notable among them the charming Free Church Girls' School), the Association rooms of the Y.M. and Y.W.C.A., and the Salvation Army barracks in the heart of the native quarter. As Father writes:—

'There is a very pleasing degree of unity and brotherly love among the missionaries in Madras. They are more thrown into each other's society than workers of different denominations at home, and the effects are excellent. We met most of them, and many of them again and again, during our stay, and felt much drawn to them as true and devoted servants of the LORD; though I cannot help regretting that in Madras City out of fifty male missionaries less than a quarter are engaged in vernacular work—or Gospel work in native languages; of the remaining three-fourths the larger number are occupied in educational work, which is done in English.'

As to their unity, no wonder, since

A MADRAS OIL-SELLER.

verily 'to men who live in a country where the people worship cows, monkeys, snakes, and even devils, anything which separates Christians is as the small dust of the balance.'

At the C.M.S. Divinity School we stayed all our time. It is a pleasant, roomy bungalow, lent in part to the friends who have so hospitably received us. The school, like the similar one we saw at Poona, is for training native catechists and preachers, who go out evangelising and return after six months or so for further Bible and theological instruction. The students' houses in the compound, a row of simple little homes, are full of pleasant-faced Christian wives and little children. The Salvation Army folk are, I am told, the only foreign workers who live among the natives in Madras. Their barracks, a large building with a good hall below and very self-denying, punkahless quarters upstairs, stand on the main street

GROUP OF NATIVE CONVERTS Z.B.M.M.

THE C.M.S. MADRAS DIVINITY SCHOOL, DEC., 1896.
(W. S. Hooton, B.A., and the Rev. H. D. Goldsmith in the centre.)

of Blacktown, a noisy, narrow, crowded thoroughfare. The climate of Madras is so trying to Europeans that every one tries to secure punkahs, compounds, space and air. But somehow the S.A. workers survive and succeed *minus* these things—well, not quite *minus* all of them, they certainly have *some* air, but it is not much, and especially cannot be much in summer. Their devotion is, I think, very real. The English officer who showed me over had been eight years in India without furlough. She looked worn and thin, but is bravely holding on. 'The Army' does the only rescue work that is done in Madras. The Home is a pleasant house in a nice neighbourhood, as it would not be wise to keep its inmates in the native quarter. I was much

touched by the pre- sent the girls there worked for me and brought up here before we left. They do a good deal of needlework, which is sold to help the funds.

In early days Blacktown was the home of other missionaries—S.P.G. and C.M.S. workers, for instance. But times have changed. The C.M.S. is only now represented in Madras by a native church, Moslem school, and by its South India secretary, Mr. Goldsmith.

The Madras Missionary Conference meets once a month. Down near the sea, on one hot winter night, we had the pleasure of attending the gathering at which Mr. Burgess, newly come out to represent the Sunday School Union throughout the Indian Empire, and Mr. Sherwood Eddy, of the Student Volunteer Movement, were received. Mr. Burgess's parish is a big one— 117 million bairns! Only 5,500 Sunday Schools are opened for these myriads of bright and active little hearts and brains; while at home for fourteen million children we have 53,590 Sunday schools. Mr. Burgess asked me to tell the home folks about the needs of the children of India. I pass on his message in the two following diagrams which represent the facts of the case— facts which speak for themselves, and plead for more earnest effort that these Indian little ones should receive the knowledge that alone can give what most we need, peace, purity, strength, and love.

Each ● = 1 million grown-up people in India.
Each ○ = 1 million Indian boys and girls (117 millions).
The whole diagram = everybody in India (300 millions).
The little dot in the middle = all the Indian boys and girls that go to Sunday School (250,000).

A Page for the Little Ones

*Hullo, over there!
Just think!
There are so many boys & girls in India, that if they all stood in a line, shoulder to shoulder & great tremendous bridges were made across the sea for them to stand on, they'd reach right round the world!
They'd make a huge immense ring, 2,500 miles long.
And only one child in each mile of that big ring, would ever have been inside a Sunday School!*

INDIAN SUNDAY SCHOOL BOYS AND GIRLS.

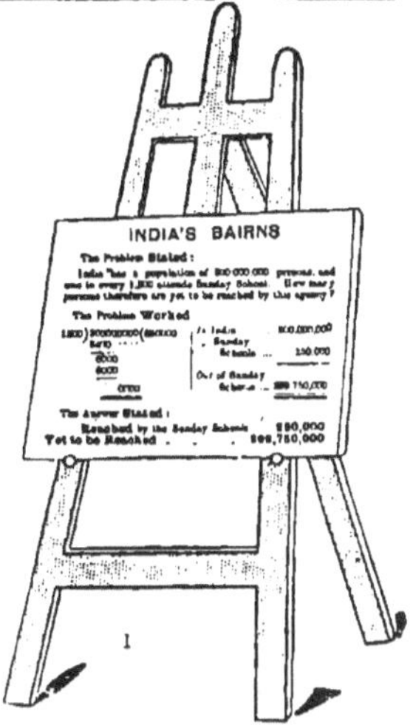

'FEED MY LAMBS.'

'Suffer little children to come unto Me, and forbid them not, for of such is the kingdom of heaven.'

Chapter XII

ASSCCIATION WORK

'FROM SHORE TO SHORE'

'There is nothing in the world worth living for but doing good and finishing God's work, doing the work that Christ did.'—BRAINERD.

WHEN, nearly 200 years ago, after an eight months' voyage from Denmark to Tranquebar, the first Protestant missionaries to India reached their destination, the Governor would scarcely allow them to land, and opposed their work in every way.

We could not help recalling that experience, and contrasting the churlishness of the powers that were with the friendliness of the powers that be, as we drove down the other day to the site of the new Madras Y.M.C.A. buildings, of which the present Governor, Sir Arthur Havelock, was about to lay the foundation stone. Very different was the position of the missionaries gathered on the platform of the spacious tent put up for the occasion and brightly decorated with flags, bunting, flowers and greenery, as they sat there waiting for his Excellency to appear, to the position of those two solitary young men whom the Governor of 1707 kept standing shelterless in the blazing sun of the town square all through the long hours of their first day in India. And very different, on those two occasions, was the speech that the Governor made. Nothing could have been more hostile than the first, nothing more cordial than the latter. Listening to it, with the great Indian Ocean stretching away to the eastern horizon just across the esplanade, our thoughts travelled over the continent to the western sea, and to the pretty oriental-looking building of the

Bombay Young Men's Association overlooking the blue waters of the Bay of Bengal.

'His Kingdom stretch from shore to shore.'

It is so. What progress in development, progress in extent, progress in recognition as a blessing to the world, has the Kingdom of CHRIST made in India since the days of Ziegenbalg!

Seven years of prayer and effort lie behind this new Madras Y.M.C.A. House. Under the active superintendence of its founder and present secretary, Mr. D. McConaughy, the Association now includes over 400 members. Of these only 260 profess to be Christians. The remainder profess various other religious beliefs, the bulk being Hindus.

'To the question,' said the president, Mr. Rierson Arbuthnot, in his interesting address to the Governor—' To the question whether, if Hindus, Mahommedans, Parsees, and others belong to the Association, we have any right to call it a Christian Association, the reply is apparent—it is not called a Christian Young Men's Association, but a Young Men's Christian Association.

'If asked to define the true position of the Madras Young Men's Christian Association, I would say that, while respecting the religious beliefs of all, and recognising the very high moral teaching contained in many systems of religion, we are fully convinced that, except the name of JESUS, "there is none other name under heaven given among men whereby we must be saved." This we endeavour to make clear to all—to professing Christians as well as to those who profess other beliefs—and to bring our members to experience the result of a heart-belief in JESUS CHRIST is the chief aim and object of the Association.'

Night by night in the beautiful lecture hall of the Christian College, kindly lent by Dr. Miller for Father's addresses to students, we have met hun-

FENN HOSTEL, MADRAS CHRISTIAN COLLEGE.

dreds of intelligent young men, educated English-speaking natives. Who can rightly estimate the importance of the work, which the Association —founded half a century ago in England, but only here since 1870—seeks to do among them? A veritable life-line flung out across the stormy waters of temptation that beset, above all in a heathen land, the bark of a young man's life, it is held by strong and loving hands, right round the world. This handsome Madras building is the gift of America and England, the site being bought for over £1,200 by Great Britain, America giving as much for the superstructure, while the Government of Madras is adding its grant-in-aid. And by similar world-wide sympathy the Association work in seventy-four leading centres has raised its half-dozen buildings, and holds an average of 120 meetings in India every week. Ten Y.M.C.A. secretaries are labouring in Lahore, Bombay, Poona, Calcutta, and Madras, addressing thousands of India's young men, 4,600 of whom have already joined as Y.M.C.A. members. The spiritual side of the work has everywhere, we rejoice to know, the first place. The athletic and educational departments, with their regular classes in which members study banking, book-keeping, shorthand, typewriting, and commer-

'A LIFE-LINE, FLUNG ACROSS THE STORMY WATERS.'

cial correspondence, and enjoy tennis, badminton, and cycling, are felt by the leaders to be of small importance compared to moral and spiritual life.

The answers to the subjoined questions, recently sent to headquarters, will interest all friends of this good work.

Q. What is the number of young men who constitute the sphere of the Association in India?

A. Estimate one-tenth of the population, *i.e.*, about thirty millions.

Q. How far does the work done cover the field you hope to reach?

A. It is deeply felt that we have scarcely begun the work in India on behalf of India's young men, for which so great a burden of responsibility rests on English Christians.

Q. What immediate extension, if any, is contemplated, and where should gifts be sent to the India department of the work?

A. A worker for Burma, and additional workers for strategic points in India.

'The woman's cause is man's; they rise or sink
Together, dwarfed or Godlike, bond or free.'

And the same Power that in the last few years has raised up the world-wide union for helping young manhood to reach the noblest life has called into being the Y.W.C.A. With an even larger membership than its fellow association, and with national organisations in Italy, Norway, Sweden, Canada, and the United States, as well as in Great Britain, this helping hand for young womanhood has lately started work in India. Only a few days after Sir Arthur Havelock had presided at the young men's gathering, Lady Havelock took the chair at an equally successful Y.W.C.A. annual meeting. Father had spoken at the first—among the dozen meetings he addressed in Madras—and I had the pleasure of taking part in the second. The memory of those

LORD KINNAIRD.
Hon. Treas. London Y.W.C.A. and Z.B. and M.M.

134 ACCOMPLISHING

A CALCUTTA Y.W. GROUP.

two crowded tents with their pretty decorations in the hot Indian sunshine, and of the pleasant 'at home' that followed, in the

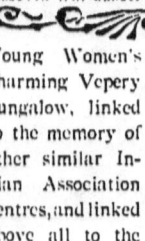

Y.W.C.A. HEADQUARTERS, CALCUTTA.
The 'Impossible' House.

Young Women's charming Vepery bungalow, linked to the memory of other similar Indian Association centres, and linked above all to the earnest Association leaders whom we met—Mr. and Mrs. Campbell White of Calcutta, the McConaughys of Madras, Mr. Frank Anderson of Bombay, and others—live in our thoughts, among the lines of light spanning and illumining India at the dawn of the twentieth century.

The effort for young women in India is twenty years old. Begun in Bombay and Poona, it has spread from Darjeeling among the Himalayan snows to Ceylon in its summer seas, has sixty-five branches and four central institutions, in Bombay, Calcutta, Darjeeling, and Madras. The story of its commencement at Calcutta is interesting.

In 1873 in a small Calcutta flat, its pioneer, Miss Orlebar, gathered 600 members. Her popular 'at homes' were over full.

THE IMPOSSIBLE

In all Calcutta no boarding-house for young women existed, and she set out to find one wherein to 'home' her lasses. One day in a pleasant quarter she lit on just the place—a Rajah's house, large, quiet, commodious, with cool marble floors, an upper storey, and good grounds.

'Oh,' said the Discouragers, who are very rarely wanting, 'you need not think you will get that! The Rajah will not let it to any but his own friends. Plenty of Europeans would like to get that house. Besides, how could you secure the rent of such a place?'

'The LORD will give us that house, if it be the right one for us to have,' was Miss Orlebar's quiet response.

'But,' every one assured her, 'there is really *no* hope of securing it! At any rate, in *Calcutta* it would be impossible to find a suitable house and compound for Y.W.C.A. work at a reasonable rental.'

'And yet,' replied the unspoken conviction in the listener's heart, 'that house and that compound I must get.'

To her the fact that they were 'not to be had' made little or no difference. She believed in the Supplier of all need.

It was the old story. On the threshold of the promised land a nation's courage fails—'It can't be done.' But there are those

MISS MORLEY,
Hon. Sec. London Y.W.C.A.

MRS. E. W. MOORE,
Hon. Sec. British National Council, Y.W.C.A.

THE HON. EMILY KINNAIRD,
Hon. Sec. London Y.W.C.A.

THE HON. LOUISA KINNAIRD.

THE HON. GERTRUDE KINNAIRD,
Hon. Sec. Zenana Bible and Medical Mission.

who know it can. And these men and these women GOD uses to accomplish the impossible.

A few days later the agent called and asked what she wanted the house for, and what rent she could give? Lifting up her heart, she named a price, considerably less than she understood others were willing to give. In a week the reply came that she could have the house, and she proceeded with the furnishing, alterations, and repairs, trusting the LORD to send the money. A heavy bill was anticipated for sanitary improvements. Three months later Miss Orlebar was leaving for meetings in the Punjab.

'If the bill comes, what shall I do?' asked the lady superintendent.

'Keep it till I return. I shall only be gone a week,' was the reply.

On her return she was greeted by—'The bill has come to 1,500 rupees!'

About noon arrived a registered letter from England containing nearly one half the required sum. During the day postal orders from India completed it within fifty rupees, and as Miss Orlebar retired to rest a guest put into her hand fifty rupees—a thank-offering for spiritual help. Thus in one day the need was supplied.

And thus in the irresistible extension of the Kingdom of JESUS CHRIST this bond of love and purity, which encircles to-day 100,000 young women in Great Britain, an equal number in America and the Colonies, and a total world-membership of about half a million, is reaching out to India. With ninety secretaries, holding some 200 meetings a week, with 3,000 members, and an annual expenditure of about £500, it has already been used to the conversion and blessing of English-speaking and Eurasian girls, and reckons as its parish '100,000 English-speaking women and many hundreds of thousands of native Christians to be reached in the vernacular.' 'It wants,' Headquarters tell me, 'ten competent local secretaries at once, and several other workers.' There is also hope of developing the work in colleges, if a suitable college secretary can be found.

The recent visits paid by Lord Kinnaird, the Hon. Misses Kinnaird and Miss Morley to India have given a great impetus to Association work. Miss Morley writes: 'We are starting a new Y.W. Institute in Bombay, where it is as much, if not more, needed as in Calcutta. Friends are generously helping, but more money is required to launch the scheme. A house, most suitably placed, near the Apollo Bunder, has been secured, and we believe the Association has already sufficient headway in Bombay to make this undertaking a success when once fairly started.'

The Y.W.C.A. in India seeks specially to reach :—

(1) European girls from home—those in business, governesses, medical students, schoolmistresses, soldiers' young wives, etc., etc.
(2) Domiciled Europeans and Eurasians.
(3) Educated native Christians.

Great possibilities lie in these young lives, and in the greater contingent of young manhood under the high influence of the Y.M.C.A. Acclimatised, knowing the country and the people, and with heart and interest ready prepared, are not they the natural evangelists of India?

BENGALI Y.W.C.A. MEMBERS

Chapter XIII
NEO-HINDUISM

'In its terror and hatred, Paganism essayed the resistance of an eclectic revival. For the old humanistic worship... it substituted a naturalistic cult, which, for an age of decaying faith, had a horrible fascination.... But the revival, with all its paraphernalia of mathematicians and jugglers, lustrations and oracles, weird exorcisms and ghastly taurobolia, was all in vain; it never succeeded in galvanising into even the semblance of life the corrupting corpse of the old religion. Great Pan was dead.'—*The Witness of History to Christ.* FARRAR.

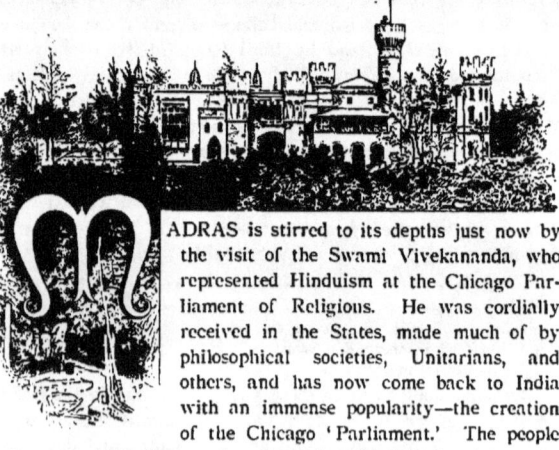

MADRAS is stirred to its depths just now by the visit of the Swami Vivekananda, who represented Hinduism at the Chicago Parliament of Religions. He was cordially received in the States, made much of by philosophical societies, Unitarians, and others, and has now come back to India with an immense popularity—the creation of the Chicago 'Parliament.' The people idolise him, believing, as he says, that Christianity is on the wane in the West, and that the millions of Great Britain and America are thirsting for the Hindu faith!

Triumphant arches were put up along the broad roads of Madras for his reception, and 10,000 people, it is said, turned out to meet him. The crowds at his lectures were at first so great that a charge was made for seats, an arrangement which half emptied the Victoria Hall, though hundreds attend his free dis-

INDIA'S LIGHT!

cussion meetings, held every morning at 7.30 in a tent by the seashore.

Oh, this poor dark India! If there is anything more pathetic than its darkness, I think it is its light. Think, in comparison with the revelation of 'the KING, eternal, immortal, invisible,' of the subjoined idea—I can find no words to characterise it —Vivekananda's notion of the evolution of GOD.

'Starting from some fungus, some very minute, microscopic bubble, and all the time drawing from that infinite storehouse of energy, the form is changed slowly and slowly, until, in course of time, it becomes a plant, then an animal, then man, ultimately God.'—*Yoga Philosophy*, p. 43.

To the great audiences that hang upon his lips he preaches human sinlessness, human divinity.

'Ye are the children of God, the sharers of immortal bliss, holy and perfect beings. Ye, divinities on earth, sinners! It is a sin to call a man so. It is a standing libel on human nature.

'The worst lie that you ever told yourself was that you were a sinner, or a wicked man.

'It is the greatest of all lies that we are men ; we are the god of the universe. We have been always worshipping our own selves.

'Thou art that (*tat twam asi*). And the whole universe of myriads of suns and moons, everything that speaks, with one voice will say, "Thou art that."'[1]

'Awakened India' hails these doctrines as inspired, and rejoicing in the triumphs of her sons in the West—Prince Ranjitsinhji leading England in her national game of cricket, Mr. A. Chatterjea first in the Indian Civil Service examination, and the researches of Professor J. C. Bose acknowledged by European scientists—ranks Vivekananda with them.

With the nihilism of Nirvana as a goal, and renunciation as the means of escaping endless rebirths, Neo-Hinduism plunges its followers into the gloom of transmigration, and the necessity of saving oneself from life and pain.

'Slay thou . . . the enemy in the form of desire. . . . Renunciation leads to the highest bliss. . . . One should neither rejoice in obtaining what is pleasant, nor sorrow in obtaining what is unpleasant. . . . Near to

---

[1] New York lecture, quoted in *The Lr. himavadin*, August 29th, 1896.

the Nirvana approach those who know themselves, who are disjoined from desire and passion . . . having cast away hope and fear. . . .

'Strive for liberation from birth and death. . . .

'Mahatmas come not again to birth. . . . He who, seated as a neutral, is unshaken . . . standeth apart, immovable, balanced in pleasure and pain, self-reliant, to whom a lump of earth, a rock and gold are alike; the same to loved and unloved, the same in censure and in praise, the same in honour and ignominy, the same to friend and foe, abandoning all undertakings, he is said to have crossed over the Gunas. . . . He wants nothing . . . neither loveth, nor hateth, nor grieveth, nor desireth, renouncing good and evil . . . destitute of attachment . . silent . . . homeless . . .'[1]

This is the ideal. There is no other hope, no other way. And there is no Hand to help in this pitiful endeavour not to be!

FAKIR BURYING HIS HEAD.
(From a photograph.)

Having become a *yogi* by these means, we may, according to the Swami, do wonders.

'The Yogi can enter a dead body and make it get up and move, even when he himself is working in another body.'

'The Yogi proposes to himself no less a task than to master the whole universe, to control the whole of nature.'

'When the Yogi becomes perfect, there will be nothing in nature not under his control. If he orders the gods to come, they will come at his bidding; if he asks the departed to come, they will come at his bidding.'[2]

These are the doctrines now being daily taught by this eloquent man. This is the faith that he proposes Hindus should

---

[1] From the *Bhagavad Gita*, part of the Hindu Scriptures.
[2] *Yoga Philosophy*, pp. 198, 11, 32.

'Go out to preach to every nation, starting institutions in India to train young men to become preachers. Strong men and sincere men are wanted. With a few hundred such the world will be revolutionised.'

'Revolutionised?' In this crowded discussion meeting this morning by the sea, I asked whether Neo-Hinduism contemplates abolishing child-marriage and cruelty to widows? His answer was negative. Though he deplores these evils, the faith he preaches has no means of remedying them. Neo-Hinduism has no message, no help for India's women.

Does it propose to abolish idolatry? No, the Swami answered, he considers idols very useful things, leading the masses, on the Kindergarten plan, step by step up to a faith in the Unseen. He would leave idolatry just as it is, only substituting for the present grotesque images more artistic statues from the West!

Looking in the faces of the 600 men, seated on the tent floor densely packed together, drinking in this sad philosophy, my heart went out to them and the millions they represent—millions who know no more than this, whose only light is here. How reachable they are we felt next morning when, coming down before breakfast to attend the early meeting, we found the Swami absent, and no one to speak to the big tent full of men. Father offered to be Swami, and answered the interesting, thoughtful questions of the audience, not only in the tent, but (when word came from headquarters that the meeting must disperse) out in the sunny highway. Quite a large group of students walked with us till we found a shady spot, and sat down together under the roadside trees. Never shall I forget that morning hour, the sun in his fresh splendour coming up over the sea, Father standing in his light things answering the puzzling questions of the students, thin palm-leaf shadows sifting over us, and the heat every moment growing greater. Never shall I lose the sense that hour gave me of the opening throughout India for work among English-speaking men, Hindus, and Moslems. That bright-faced, interested group of college fellows, many of them, no doubt, from the Madras Christian College, which alone has 1,800 students, was so eager, so apparently earnest, so intelligent, so lost in philosophic fog!

Oh, for the privilege of going back to work for India's students! GOD grant that some who read these lines may become His messengers to them!

A few hours later, at the Swami's invitation, we called at the Ice House, where he was staying, and, in a cool, circular room overlooking the blue sea, had an interesting chat. As Father writes:—

'We found him an avowed Pantheist, but at the same time a believer in Indian idol worship. To him everything was god and everything might be worshipped. He himself was god. He never prayed, why should he? Christianity, in his opinion, was a mass of fables derived from Buddhism and Babylonianism. The morality of Christ was excellent, but so was that of the Hindus. In all religions there were good and bad men. The highest form of religion was self-denial, self-repression, asceticism. There was no such thing as sin. How could there be when man himself was god? All forms of idolatry were defensible; they might change with time, but their right to existence remained, and idolatry would continue while the world lasted.'

His message is just the old Hindu philosophy, dissociated from the degraded features of actual Hinduism. But as was recently well said, 'What India needs is not a resuscitated metaphysics, but a new moral life, the result of getting into right relation with God, which is religion.'

'In Thy light shall we see light.'

'THE HIGHEST FORM OF RELIGION' —A HINDU ASCETIC.
(*From a photograph taken at Ajmere.*)
'The devotee, who was faithfully served by the two attendants seen beside him, had held his arms up till they were as rigid as two pieces of wood.'
India and Malaysia. THOBURN.

LIFE, NOT METAPHYSICS

Not by the candle of philosophy, not by the will o' the wisp of speculation, but by the clear beam of revelation alone can the heart be illuminated and transformed. India's moral history is an age-long proof of this. For what is it but one vast demonstration of the failure of the subtlest human thought to meet man's need? Ramabai puts the whole case into a single picture:—

'A superficial knowledge of the philosophies and religious books of India has been misleading many Western people to think that the Hindus are the sole possessors of superior spirituality. I am not surprised that the good men and women of the West, who only see the outside of the grand structures of oriental philosophy, are charmed with them.

'But the facts of the case remind me of the sight I saw at the Agra fort in the palaces of the Moghul emperors. The guide showed us the Rani's private rooms, the gardens and grand marble buildings once occupied by the kings and queens. He also showed us the beautiful pleasure - tower called Saman Burj. Visitors are shown all that is beautiful there, and they go away carrying very pleasant impressions of Agra with them. I was not satisfied with seeing the outside beauty of these "poems

'POEMS IN MARBLE.'

in marble," but wished to see the dungeons, and the place where the unfortunate women used to be confined and hanged at the pleasure of the king. The guide at first denied the existence of such places in the palace; but, finally, on obtaining a promise to get a little more money for his trouble, he consented to show the dungeons. He opened a trap-door on one side of the palace, and showed us the many small and large underground rooms where the queens who had incurred the king's displeasure used to be shut up, tortured, and starved, until it pleased his majesty to set them free. At the furthest end of the prison was a room underneath the Saman Burj, or Jasmine Tower, with a deep, dark pit in the centre, and a big beam placed on the walls right over it. This beam, beautifully carved, served for hanging the unfortunate women who once occupied the throne of the king as his queens, but had by some cause fallen under his displeasure. Their lifeless bodies were let down into that dark pit, whence a stream carried them to the waters of the Jumna, to be eaten by crocodiles. Thus the poor, miserable wives of the Moghul emperors suffered torture and death in that dark hell-pit under the pleasure-gallery, while their cruel masters and rivals sang songs, enjoyed life, and made merry over their grave. I think but little of those lovely palaces, but remember that dark room, and compare it with similar places of torture which exist in many sacred towers of India. If the walls of that horrible room had the power of speech, oh, what stories of human cruelty and misery would they tell to-day!

'I beg of my Western sisters not to be satisfied with looking on the outside beauty of the grand philosophies, and not to be charmed with hearing the

'THEY SEND OUT EMISSARIES—'

long and interesting discourses of our educated men, but to open the trap-doors of the great monuments of ancient Hindu intellect, and enter into the dark cellars, where they will see the real workings of the philosophies which they admire so much. Let our Western friends come to India, and live right among us. Let them frequently go to the hundreds of sacred places where countless pilgrims throng yearly. Let them go round Jagannath Puri, Benares, Gaya, Allahabad, Muttra, Bindraban, Dwarka, Pandharpur, Udipi, Tirpatty, and such other sacred cities, the strongholds of Hinduism and seats of sacred learning, where the Mahatmas and Sadhus dwell, and where the "sublime" philosophies are daily taught and followed.

'TO LOOK FOR YOUNG WIDOWS AND BRING THEM—'

There they will find that the men who boast superior Hindu spirituality oppress widows and trample the poor under their heels. They have deprived the widows of their birthright to enjoy pure life and lawful happiness. They send out hundreds of emissaries to look for young widows, and bring them by thousands to the sacred cities to rob them of their money and their virtue. The so-called sacred places—those veritable hells on earth—have become the graveyards of countless widows and orphans, but not a philosopher or Mahatma has come out boldly to champion their cause.

'The teachers of false philosophies and lifeless spiritualities will do no good to our people. Nothing has been done by them to protect the fatherless and judge the widow. If anything has been done by anybody at all, it has been done by those who have come under direct influence of Christianity. Education and philosophy are powerless before caste rules and priestcraft.

'I earnestly beg the women of America and England to come to India and live in our sacred cities—not in European fashion, but living like the poor, going in and out of their dirty huts, hearing the stories of their miserable lives, and *seeing the fruits of the sublime philosophies.*'

Chapter XIV
DOOMED, BUT STILL DOMINANT

The duty of all Christians towards missions has been summed up in these words: 'Go. Let go. Help go.'

HINDUISM, new and old, is perishing; must perish. The Light of the World has come. The revival we are witnessing in India in the Brahmo Somaj, the Arya Somaj, and other Reform Societies, and in Neo-Hinduism as proclaimed by its apostle Vivekananda, is a result of Christian preaching, the defence of a failing cause, like the death struggle of Paganism in the Roman Empire before the triumph of the Cross. Even in the height of his popularity with the Hindu world at his feet, the Swami shows a strange foreboding of ultimate failure. At the close of one of his addresses at the Victoria Hall, speaking on patriotism, on the need of a struggle to support the old faith, he concluded with an illustration of which the following is the gist:—

'The Indian nation has been for centuries carried from the shores of time to the shores of eternity by the great national ferry of the Hindu system and the Hindu faith. That ship has taken over generation after generation of human beings to the pleasant lands of future life. But now the ship is old, she is riddled with holes and in danger of sinking. We are on board. As patriots and as men, what is our duty? We must mend up our old vessel. With our heart's blood we must do this work, we must put our brains, our very beings into it. But shall we succeed? I come to you, my children, to help in this task. If you receive me, I will work with you; if you reject me, I shall come back and tell you—"We are all sinking; let me sit in your midst, and let us sink together."'

I cannot give you an adequate impression of the effect, but sitting there at twilight in the large half-lighted hall, it seemed like listening to the cry of a perishing faith, watching the death struggle of a doomed idolatry.

Yes, it must perish, though the fight is slow and long. And it deserves to perish. How can a system that, in spite of all its earnest, sincere, and pitiful feeling in the darkness after GOD, is yet so impure that literally half of some of its best works has to be omitted by women studying the language; [4] that to translate one of them, the *Yajurveda*, exposes the translator to punishment under the Indian Penal Code; and that Max Müller in his *Sacred Books of the East* was obliged to suppress long sections as unfit

A TEMPLE COURT AT LITTLE CONJEEVERAM.

to be read—how can this system survive contact with the white light of CHRIST?

Close to us here in Madras is the crowded 'sacred' city of Conjeeveram, which, with its 45,000 people, has never to this hour had a Christian missionary. Father went there and found it a black focus of idolatry.

'It is,' he writes, 'a city with forty-five thousand people and five hundred temples, some of them of immense size and considerable antiquity. Idolatry reigns with absolute supremacy. The Brahman is master of every mind and conscience in the place. The chief objects worshipped are obscene representations, too immoral to describe; no less than forty houses of prostitution are connected with one of the chief temples, and how many with them all I have no conception. When climbing the great tower of one of these temples hundreds of vampire bats flew round us, startled by our presence into activity. I thought the fact most typical of the character of the place, a home of moral vampires!

'There has been a mission-school in Conjeeveram for fifty years, but it has not made a convert. I spoke there twice, and on the second occasion, the public being admitted, the Gospel message was opposed at the close and jeered at, many of the mission scholars wildly applauding the opposition. Education has not succeeded in delivering any of these people from their errors The fact is most instructive. *A different power is needed, that which can raise the dead.*

'The grip which idolatry has on the mind of the ordinary Hindu is of surprising strength. Standing on the broad flight of temple steps, on either side of which a quantity of idols were displayed in the shape of cobras cut in stone, I reasoned through an interpreter with a crowd of natives on the sin and folly of idol worship, and on the character of GOD, and the nature of the

'THE FOLLY OF WORSHIPPING COBRAS CUT IN STONE.'

worship due to Him. One after another the most intelligent men in the crowd came forward to defend idolatry with an earnestness worthy of a better cause. They seemed fascinated by the lie which had been taught them as truth from their earliest years, and unable to admit a single idea conflicting with their idolatrous beliefs.'

How wide is the reign of this darkness at the close of our nineteenth century? A thousand miles along this eastern sea lies the Madras Presidency, with its inland regions swept bare by famine, its long line of Eastern Ghauts, and its green fertile coast lands stretching from Cape Cormorin up to Orissa. First to be occupied for CHRIST in modern times, Madras has been the scene of marked progress. Over 860,000 native Christians were here in 1891—1 in 40 of the population at that time. It has some well-worked districts, among them Palamcotta, set down in the recently issued S.V.M.U. *Appeal for India* as 'fully occupied.' In Travancore the L.M.S. alone reports 400 congregations, and 54,000 people; while in the Telugu country, north of Madras City, the American Baptist 'Lone Star Mission' flings out its beam of light around the world. But these are little sections. North of the Lone Star Mission scarcely one-tenth of the population is reached. One worker to 100,000 or 300,000 people; a solitary worker to a county; such is the state of things in Arcot, Negapatam (Tanjore), and other districts; while thousands of villages are practically virgin soil. Even Tinnevelly, with its population of Christians numbering five per cent., with hundreds of entirely Christian villages, and 100,000 Christians, still needs many workers, and has 'many

WOMAN OF TRAVANCORE.

'A CROWDED SACRED CITY . . . WITH A LARGE INFLUX OF PILGRIMS, BUT NO PREACHER OF JESUS CHRIST.'

purely heathen towns without either Christian or missionary.' Conjeeveram, daily defiled by sin in the name of worship, has a large influx of pilgrims, but no preacher of JESUS CHRIST. Where are the men GOD is calling to this post?

I have tried to represent on the accompanying map not only some of the chief needs of this Presidency but also of BERAR and the CENTRAL PROVINCES. Whole counties in the former, whole districts in the latter, wait in this year of grace 1898, without one messenger of JESUS CHRIST.

Think of it! Another night is gathering its darkness around Berar—a country larger than Switzerland and with more people, but heathen, heathen, heathen, north, south, and east and west. The workers there, making the lowest estimate, appeal for forty helpers, medical, evangelistic, educational, industrial, literary. Why are you settling down to be a doctor or a teacher, a writer or a preacher here at home? Berar, with its undulating valleys of black soil, the home of the cotton plant, and the heart of the cotton trade of India, though one of the smaller Indian provinces, occupies seven pages of closely printed matter in Dr. George Smith's condensed *Geography of India*. Have you ever given it even a thought? Did you even know its name until you read this paragraph?

Yet it may be that CHRIST means you to seek His lost ones there.

The wide CENTRAL PROVINCES—as large as Italy and England—lie north, above BERAR. Parched and swept bare by the famine during the last sad years, they have for untold centuries suffered the deeper hunger. Here 'the mass of the people is practically untouched.' Districts of 400,000 to 700,000 have no one, or a solitary worker. Nearly all the native States about RAIPORE are still unoccupied. In the great section of INDORE the Canadian Presbyterians have 5,000,000 to reach—about 150,000 to each of their labourers. But Indore is well worked compared to MANDLA district, where among two millions there are five labourers. Each agent of the Central India Hill Mission has a parish of 400 square miles, as if one man were set to evangelise the whole of Bedfordshire, and that under a blazing Indian sun with the slenderest resources. CHANDA, a district of over 10,000 square miles (the whole of Montenegro has only 2,000 or 3,000 square miles), with 2,700 villages and over 600,000 people, has but one missionary. Gold is found in the sand of its hill streams; north and south it is rich in iron ore; rubies and diamonds have been dug from its mines; teak forests cover its hillsides, rising

ON THE KAHAN RIVER, INDORE.

high on the eastern frontier. Is there no wealth of hearts and lives more precious in the sight of GOD than these things we have sought and found in Chanda? To seek its men and women, why should not you go?

BHANDARA, with rugged granite rocks, the lake region of the Central Provinces, has 3,600 sheets and tanks of water (when the rains have fallen well) dammed off and used for irrigation. Its people are 'noted for discourtesy and loose morals.' But why not? Only one man has been sent to evangelise its 4,000 square miles and 700,000 souls. 'How shall they believe on Him of whom they have not heard?' 'Phallic worship is universal' in Bhandara. Near one of the villages the tomb of an Englishwoman is venerated. Why not—things being as they are?

WARDHA, the next district, famous for its buffaloes and cotton growing; BALAGHAT, with its waste highland plateau, its peaks 2,000 to 3,000 feet high, and its teak and bamboo forests, lie near, each with one worker only—well off in having him. Wardha is as large as Lancaster; Balaghat as Bedfordshire and Devonshire together.

Are you tired of these names? There are so many. They are so strange to us. But though we may forget them, not one of them is forgotten before GOD.

And it may be that as we kneel to pray to-night we shall feel dull and cold, almost as if we were not near Him. And it may be that the reason of the weakness of our prayer is our disobedience, our neglect.

'You come to us,' exclaims the Hindu Vivekananda, 'you come to us with your religion of yesterday—to us who were taught thousands of years ago by our Rishis precepts as noble as your CHRIST's; you trample on us and treat us as the dust beneath your feet; you destroy life in our animals; you degrade our people with drink; you scorn our religion, in many points like your own; and then you wonder why Christianity makes such slow progress in India. I tell you *it is because you are not like your Christ*. Do you think if you came to our doors like Him, meek and lowly, with a message of love, living and working and suffering for others as He did, we should turn a deaf ear? Oh no! We should receive Him and listen to Him.'

It is true. To nine-tenths of India we have nationally misrepresented Christianity, and we have not yet brought CHRIST.

ORISSA.

AN INDIAN BRIDE.

'He who listens to the words of a woman will be accounted worthless.'

'If the word woman be uttered, even a demon will be moved with compassion.'

'No matter how skilled a woman may be in numbers and letters, her judgment will be second-rate."

—*Tamil Proverbs.*

Missionary. — 'You take a stone; half of it you make into a doorstep and the other half into a god!'

Hindu. — 'True, but there are my mother and my wife — both women. I respect the one and beat the other!'

IN THE WOMEN'S QUARTERS.

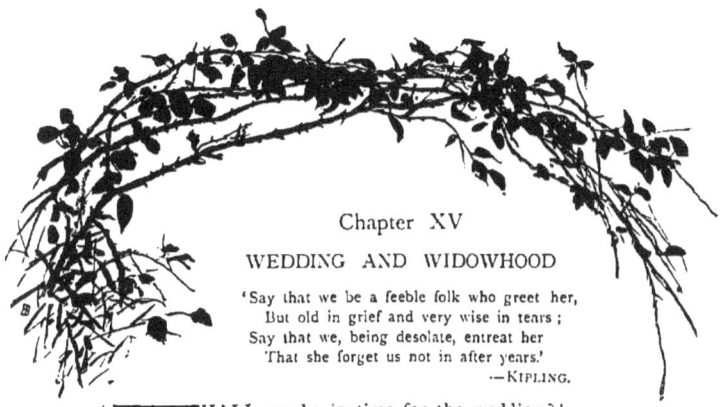

Chapter XV
WEDDING AND WIDOWHOOD

'Say that we be a feeble folk who greet her,
But old in grief and very wise in tears ;
Say that we, being desolate, entreat her
That she forget us not in after years.'
—KIPLING.

'SHALL we be in time for the wedding?'
'Well, as it lasts for several days, we shall certainly be in time for something ; but I should like you to see the procession.'

The doctor put his turbaned head out of the *gari* window to urge our driver faster along the darkening street.

'Ah, it's all right,' he added, facing round on me. 'They have not started. See!'

I looked out and down the dusky road. The way was blocked ahead of us by a dense crowd of people—shouting, music, noise, stopped vehicles. My friend alighted, and left me wondering and expectant. Somehow a special interest attaches to a wedding, be it where it may. I sat in the twilight waiting. Indian stars came out overhead in the deep blue. Was the bride's heart beating high on this her marriage day?

'It is all right, Miss Guinness; they have delayed for us. Let me introduce you to the bridegroom's father.'

The doctor's cheery voice broke in upon my reverie. A Hindu gentleman outside the carriage door bowed courteously, helped me to alight, and swiftly piloted us down into the heart of the *tamasha*.

What an Eastern scene it is!—flaming lamps, candles, and scintillating lights in coloured bowls held high above the bearers' heads, lining both sides of the procession; a central phalanx of brilliantly dressed ladies, relatives of the family, on foot and packed into a solid square—their faces turned towards us as we pass, dozens of large dark eyes and shining polished *coiffures* of black hair, dozens of sleek brown arms and necks loaded with jewellery, and draped in delicate silk *saris*. It is a proud moment for the master of the ceremonies, who makes way for us through the festive throng.

AMID THE ADMIRING WONDER OF THE CROWD.

The noise around is deafening. Beating of drums and blare of native music almost prevent our hearing his explanations of the next feature of the show —a tiny girl and boy covered with silks and jewellery, seated on two gaily-bedizened horses, led by attendants at the very slow foot pace of the moving multitude. The noise grows louder as, with a glance at the children's pretty faces grave with the solemnity of so great an occasion, we are piloted through a

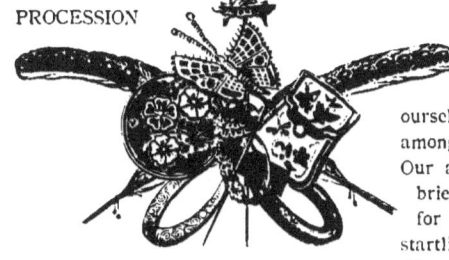

densely-crowded part of the procession, and find ourselves in the front ranks among the musicians who lead. Our advent is the signal for a brief pause in the march, and for the execution of specially startling music by an indescribable performer.

What words will represent the rattling noise, the *furore*, the contortions, the frenzy of music that succeeds? Under the eye of the father-in-law and of the white-faced stranger the player's enthusiasm reaches a climax. Higher and higher waxes the excitement, amid the admiring wonder of the crowd, until at last, with a final deafening burst, he suddenly subsides, and another musician steps forward.

Scent is showered from costly ornamented vases. Some one behind brings a beautiful garland of flowers, which the courteous master of affairs places with much ceremony around my neck. The wreath—a boa of flowers—is closely woven of lovely tropical bloom, heavy with scent, and falling below the waist. I express what thanks are possible amid the din of bagpipe music. We step into the carriage, and are swiftly bowed away, leaving the *tamasha* creeping down the street amid the flare of torchlight and prodigal showers of scent.

It is in progress from the bride's

A NINE-YEAR-OLD WIFE

INDIAN BRIDE AND BRIDEGROOM.

house to the bridegroom's, and will arrive in due course at the pleasant residence where in a few moments we alight, and mount the steps.

Oh, she is such a little bride! You stand hushed in her presence, scarcely able to believe that this is really she.

In the central room of the house she sits on a cushion by the bridegroom, both of them cross-legged on the floor. The women of the household, in gay gowns and solemn silence, are seated on the floor behind. Hindu musicians in front are performing soft, weird music. Delicate refreshments are laid in a side room. The little bride is eight years old, a tiny, shy slip of a child; the husband a tall, vigorous young man of about twenty. He speaks English well, and talks freely to me, but does not move from his place upon the floor.

Her uncle picks up the little bride in his arms, as you might a child of two, and carries her off into the refreshment room, to try and get her to say a few words to me; but she is too shy to utter anything but her name, which comes out at last, after much persuasion. Some one carries a small boy past, dressed in the brightest scarlet. The wee bride stretches out her hand to him; they are evidently playmates.

'She is more fit for that little five-year-old than for the bridegroom you are giving her,' I remark pitifully.

A BRIDE OF EIGHT.
'They beat me because I cried for my mother.'

'Ah, *Mem Sahib*, no! Such age is not our custom.'

The age that *is* the custom, is painfully evident. Everything around you is pretty, shining, gay with music, and lit by a glare of light; but oh, it is so sad! As you realise what this wedding represents, you feel that you have scarcely ever seen anything sadder than this wee bride in her green silk dress and costly ornaments—a mite encrusted in a load of jewels. In two years she will be actually married to this full-grown man.

But this, after all, is little. It might have been far worse, since Indian custom demands that every decent family should secure husbands for its girls while they are young—in their cradles, five, eight, or ten years of age—and the age of the husband does not matter.

It frequently happens that girls of eight or nine are given to men of sixty or seventy. The younger they are married the better, 'the greater is the merit, thereby the parents are entitled to rich rewards in heaven.'

A sense of the suffering of India's 143 million women and girls comes over me as I look at the tiny bride.

'Will that child be actually married in two years?' I ask my native friend.

'Yes,' he answers.

'But she is not fit; it is cruel; it will injure her.'

'*Very much*,' he answers emphatically; 'very much so indeed. But they dare not resist. Their mothers instruct them that they must submit.' And the doctor goes on to tell me pitiful cases of suffering among girls whom, as a medical man, he had been called to try and relieve.

One cannot write of these things, but they make one realise the cry of India's women. No wonder that the nation is weak; that it is 'sinking,' as Vivekananda said.

* * * * *

We are shown round the galleries of the decorated house

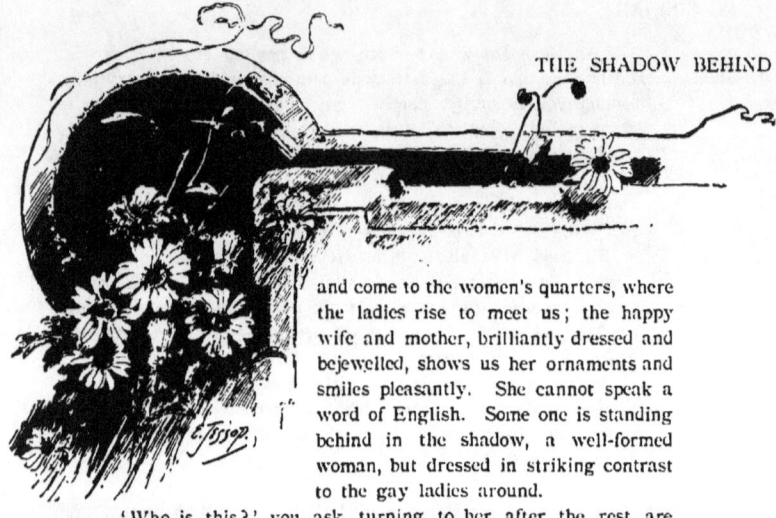

THE SHADOW BEHIND

and come to the women's quarters, where the ladies rise to meet us; the happy wife and mother, brilliantly dressed and bejewelled, shows us her ornaments and smiles pleasantly. She cannot speak a word of English. Some one is standing behind in the shadow, a well-formed woman, but dressed in striking contrast to the gay ladies around.

'Who is this?' you ask, turning to her after the rest are introduced.

'Ah, she is a widow!' comes the grave and sad response.

No more need be said. You see she wears no ornaments and stands in plain, dull clothing, distinct from all the others. And the words of the Hindu catechism recur to you strangely:—

Q. What is cruel?
A. The heart of a viper.
Q. What is more cruel than that?
A. The heart of a woman.
Q. What is the cruellest of all?
A. The heart of a sonless, penniless widow.

Widowhood in India is not only a life-long sorrow, but a life-long curse. It is believed to be the effect of some horrible crime committed by the woman in a previous life, a crime for which her husband has been punished. He has died, but she must suffer. Of course! It is her fault.

The widow must wear a single coarse garment, white, red, or brown. She must eat only one meal during the twenty-four hours of a day. She must never

THE BRIDAL FLOWERS

take part in family feasts with others. She must not show herself on auspicious occasions. People think it unlucky to behold a widow's face before seeing any other object in the morning. A man will postpone his journey if his path happen to be crossed by a widow at the time of his departure. The relatives and neighbours of the young widow's husband are always ready to call her bad names, and to address her in abusive language at every opportunity. There is scarcely a day of her life on which she is not cursed by these people as the cause of their beloved friend's death.

Hindu women, whose heads are shaved on becoming widows, think it worse than death to lose their beautiful hair. Look at this little lassie, only fourteen years old, her eyes swollen with bitter tears, sitting with a sad face out of everybody's way. She hardly knows the reason why her hair has been cut off, or why she is so cruelly deprived of all her much-loved ornaments. She will grow up in this sadness—grow up, perhaps, to feel inarticulately what a Hindu widow wrote:—

O Lord, hear my prayer! No one has turned an eye on the oppression that we poor women suffer, though with weeping and crying and desire we have turned to all sides, hoping that some one would save us. No one has lifted up his eyelids to look upon us, nor inquire into our case. We have searched above and below, but Thou art the only One who wilt hear our complaint; Thou knowest our impotence, our degradation, our dishonour.

O great Lord! our name is written with drunkards, with lunatics, with imbeciles, with the very animals; as they are not responsible we are not. Criminals confined in the jails for life are happier than we, for they know

HIGH-CASTE CHILD WIVES.

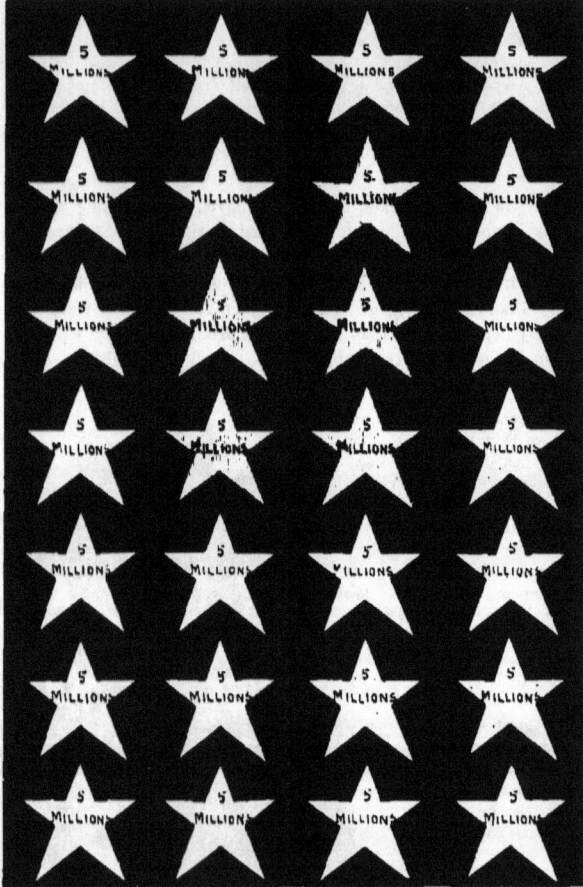

DIAGRAM REPRESENTING THE 145,000,000 WOMEN AND GIRLS OF INDIA.
Each star represents 5,000,000 women and girls.
The five shaded central stars represent India's 25 MILLION WIDOWS.

something of Thy world. They were not born in prison, but we have not for one day—no, not even in our dreams—seen Thy world. To us it is nothing but a name; and not having seen the world, we cannot know Thee, its Maker. Those who have seen Thy works may learn to understand Thee, but for us, who are shut in, it is not possible to learn to know Thee. We see only the four walls of the house. Shall we call them the world, or India? We have been born in this jail, we have died here, and are dying.

The Indian woman as a bride goes inside her husband's house, and never or scarcely ever goes out again till she is carried out to be buried. For the rest of her life she is hidden there in a living tomb. And if she be a widow that tomb becomes a prison-house of pain, from which unnumbered cries, such as that we have just read, go up to God.

But we know all about it. We have heard so very often. Books have been written, and thousands of speeches made about India's women.

And we know the figures—huge figures moving among millions —145,000,000 women; 25,000,000 widows, 77,000 of them little girls under ten years old; over 5,000,000 shut up in zenanas, most of whom have never even heard the name of Christ.

Yes, we know the figures, and we have a general notion that plenty of good people are doing all that need be done for India's women. Thank God, good work is being done by thirty-four Societies, with over 700 agents all told—700 to reach 145,000,000, over 200,000 apiece. But at least 130,000,000 of India's women can never yet have heard of woman's Friend.

* * * * *

He sat once by the wayside, not thinking about millions—about one. He was very tired, but not too tired to care about her sorrows, her shame; to talk to her, to bring her home to God.

And we, amid life's many claims, who say we follow Him, have we cared yet for 'one of these' in India, as Jesus cared that day?

Chapter XVI
CALCUTTA AND BENGAL

Providential guidance and admonition from within, and thirst and appetite not addressed to the objects which this world furnishes and provides, but reaching far beyond it, and an ambition . . . of a very different quality from the commodity ordinarily circulated under that name, something irrepressible, something mysterious and invisible, prompted and guided this remarkable man to the scene of his labours. Upon that scene he stands in competition, I rejoice to think, with many admirable, holy, saintly men . . . the noble army of the confessors of Christ.
GLADSTONE.

TO be out on the quiet yet breezy waters of the Indian Ocean is delightful after the hot-house climate of Madras. Father, after his meetings, feels revived already, and, when the almost terribly glorious sun has set, luxuriates in the starry depths of the southern heavens, the distant realms we saw from the Madras Observatory, where, as he says,—

'The Astronomer Royal showed us many wonders— Neptune pacing slowly on the outskirts of the Solar system, a little star among stars too minute from distance to be visible to the naked eye; Jupiter, radiant in all the glory of moons and belts, exquisitely defined in outlines and colours; star-clusters in Argo, and the great nebula in Doradus, overwhelming in magnitude, multiplicity of detail, and starry contents, — and these but specimens of the wealth of wonders in the tropical southern skies.'

INDIA'S IMMENSITY

Madras is far behind us now, a sunny dream, and for three days we have been steaming steadily north, up the 1,100 miles of coast between Calcutta and Madras. Yet this is but a section only — not a third of the whole coast-line of this vast Empire!

These lines sketched out here give you some conception of the immensity of India. North to south, from Cashmere to Colombo, the distance is as far as from London to Constantinople, *plus* a run from St. Petersburg to Rome; and east to west from Karachi, in Sind, to Mandalay, in Burma, is as far!

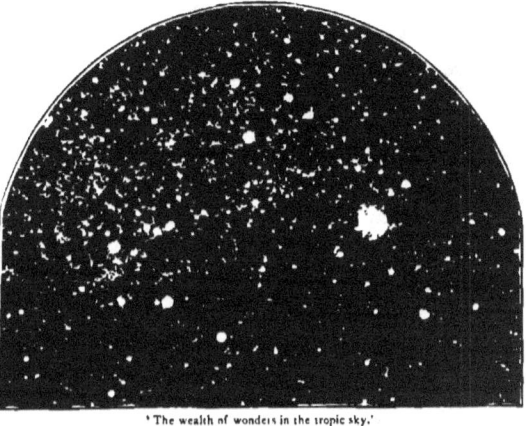

'The wealth of wonders in the tropic sky.'
A STAR PHOTOGRAPH.

*   *   *   *

We are just landing in Calcutta. The deck is in a turmoil of ropes and Lascars, baggage and bairns, passengers and afternoon tea, deck-chairs and umbrellas and farewells. Particularly umbrellas, since, wonderful to say, it is raining! All day long we have been slowly coming up the Hooghly, and might, especially at first, have been coming

up the Thames — grey, turbid, dirty-looking water; grey, heavy, cheerless skies; and rain and mist and a cold wind that felt so much like home. India might have been far away, and we landing in London on an April day, as far as one could tell. But later on shores came in view, with palm-trees, that dispelled the illusion, and now we are up in some sort of dock about three miles, they say, from the city.

'Oh, father, I am writing—I don't want to stir an inch!'

'My dear, I can't allow you to sit here within reach of that straining hawser. If it snapped, the rebound would break a man's leg easily!'

How delightful it is to be taken care of! My Singapore chair slips along the deck under dear inexorable hands, till it finds a corner among piles of luggage out of the way of the great rope by which the ship is being pulled ashore. Little children clinging to their mothers' skirts are trotting about, looking up with fascinating smiles. This waiting time seems endless. The Hooghly is so silted up with sand-banks that it was quite a question if we should get in to-night. We passed the City of Canterbury, a fine vessel, completely under water, only the top of her masts showing. She went aground in January on one of the treacherous quicksands of which the river is full. Her weight sank her when the tide was low, and when it rose she could not get free. Inch by inch the sands are swallowing her up, as they have so many others here—what a picture, what a picture!

We are nearing the shore, a low green shore, with carriages and *garis* standing waiting in the rain, and a straggling crowd of English folk and natives, among whom wait relations and friends come to meet this boat from home. Two wee boys are clinging to the taffrail calling, 'Dada! Dada! Dada!' to some Englishman below. The mother leans over looking down. How much these meetings must mean!

*   *   *   *   *

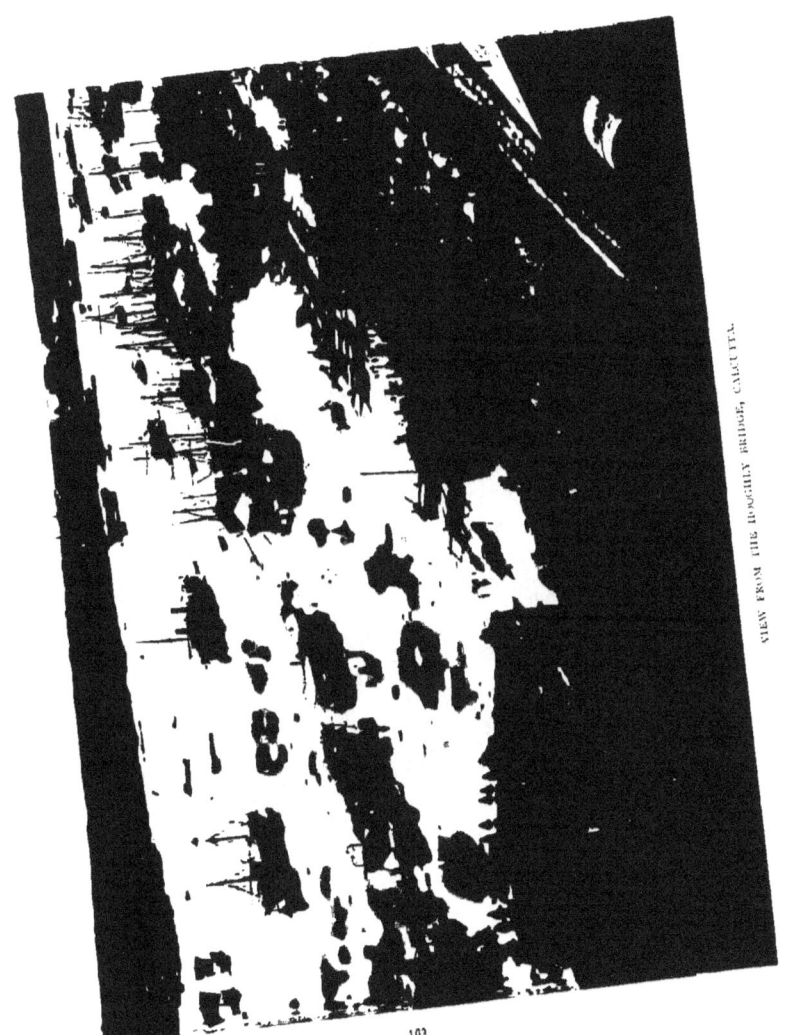

VIEW FROM THE HOOGHLY BRIDGE, CALCUTTA.

COURT HOUSE STREET, CALCUTTA.

SHADES OF A GLOOMY PAST

Calcutta . pop., 1,000,000
New Zealand „ 739,000
Glasgow „ 705,000

THE POST OFFICE, CALCUTTA.

A two miles drive up Garden Reach brings us to the heart of Calcutta — the great thronged, busy city, with its one million people, the capital of India, and of the Eastern World. Two hundred years ago a little Indian village stood on the spot where now Calcutta stands, the village of Kalcutta, called after Kali, the fierce, devouring goddess, to whose blood-stained shrine, Kali Ghat by the Hooghly, tens of thousands of worshippers still repair. The wide steps by the water are crowded with bathers at festival times, and sacrifice goes on continually, though. not the sacrifice of other days.[15] Memories of ages of horrid Kali worship linger around the spot. And memories of old-time atrocity are here too, though they seem forgotten. Where the English stifled in the Black Hole of Calcutta the magnificent buildings of the Post Office now stand. Nothing is left but history to tell the awful tale.

Calcutta to-day is modern. Government House and Town Hall, Courts and Treasury, the splendid open Maidan, the beautiful riverside drive—these and the crowded business streets with their handsome public buildings, impress one as belonging to a city that might be anywhere, built yesterday. But the crowded Dharmtolla, the Lal Bazaar and the teeming native quarters speak of a different world.

Amid the noise and hurrying of these narrow streets our *gari* rattles past an open gateway. We catch a glimpse of a quiet garden, and a white-pillared building standing among trees, old-fashioned, stately and yet simple, a refreshing contrast to the noisy neighbourhood. The name above the door, 'Lal Bazaar Baptist Chapel,' has a missionary sound. We stop the *gari* driver and pass in among the trees, little thinking that William Carey built this church, and that we shall find his chair and pulpit in the vestry—a little spindly chair and narrow pulpit, only fit for a small, light man. The present Baptist pastor very kindly takes us round, showing us the handsome silver Communion service presented by the Government of those days to Carey in recognition of his public work, and still more interesting to missionary hearts—the baptistery in which Adoniram Judson, the apostle of Burma, was baptised. It is a large oblong tank cut in the floor of the old meeting-house behind the present chapel — the very hall where Carey preached, with his and Judson's simple memorial tablets let into the wall behind the platform.

Judson's baptism in 1812—what a scene, what a seed! From this simple baptistery and from that day's doing sprang the Baptist Missionary Union of America — numbering now one million members, the evangelisation of the Karen nation, the 54,000 converts of the Telugu Lone Star Mission. The first baptising in the latter, when 2,222 former heathen were immersed in one day, nineteen years ago, and the winning of the Karens were hidden in this seed.

Thinking many thoughts we pass out into the sunshine and down the quiet path. Beyond us lies the crowded street. Pause here a moment with us at the gates of Carey's church. More than 100 years have passed since William Carey landed on Indian soil—the father of our century of missions, the first of modern Indian missionaries—more than a century of prayer and toil, of missionary appeal, and of the Church's answer to the cry

At the Gates of Carey's Church.

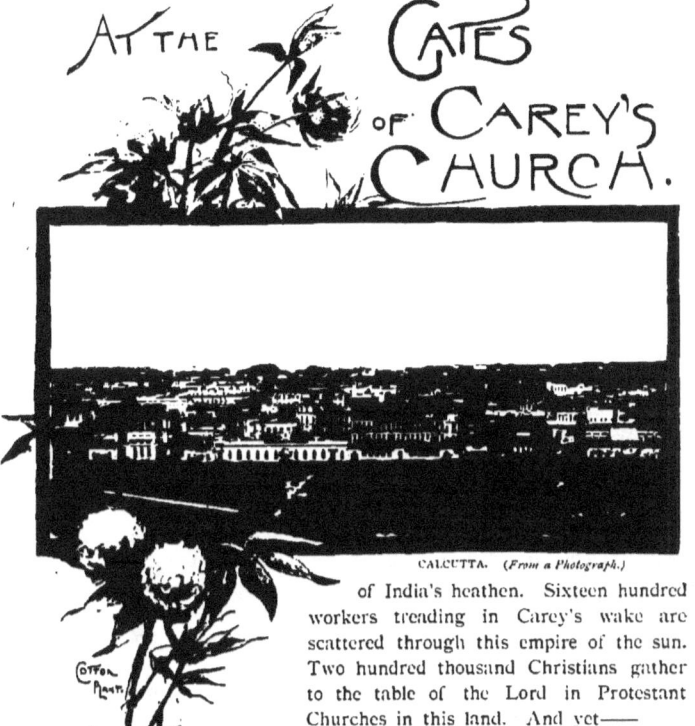

CALCUTTA. *(From a Photograph.)*

of India's heathen. Sixteen hundred workers treading in Carey's wake are scattered through this empire of the sun. Two hundred thousand Christians gather to the table of the Lord in Protestant Churches in this land. And yet——

Walk down the little garden. It is not far away, the living stream that flows by the gates of the old church ground. Look at this sight a little—the men and women here, hundreds and thousands of them passing and passing by, peasants, farmers,

DACCA.

tradesfolk, students, men of business, lawyers, merchants, doctors, all in their Indian dress. Thousands of dark eyes scan you. Keen faces, handsome faces, sensual faces — they look at you and pass. They are worshippers of Kali, the bloodthirsty destroyer; of Siva, god of death. Perhaps they may have heard the name of Christ. They may. But others have not who are not far away.

Standing here by the iron gates, with Carey's church behind you, watching this human river sweep ceaselessly by, extend your inner vision to the great plains of Bengal lying around you, from the Sunderbunds at the Ganges' mouth to the foot of the Himalayas, and from the Burman frontier to the North-West Provinces—BENGAL and ASSAM with their eighty millions, the most populous part of the world. In BAKHARGANG, at the Ganges' mouth, two great districts with 800,000 people are, as we stand here, without a missionary.[1] DACCA district is 'practically unoccupied.' Its central town has six workers among

---

[1] There are in Bakhargang several European workers and a number of native agents, but 'the whole island of Bhola is without a missionary, a native preacher, or even a Christian school. And the same may be said of Patnakali. In other words, half the district is practically untouched.'

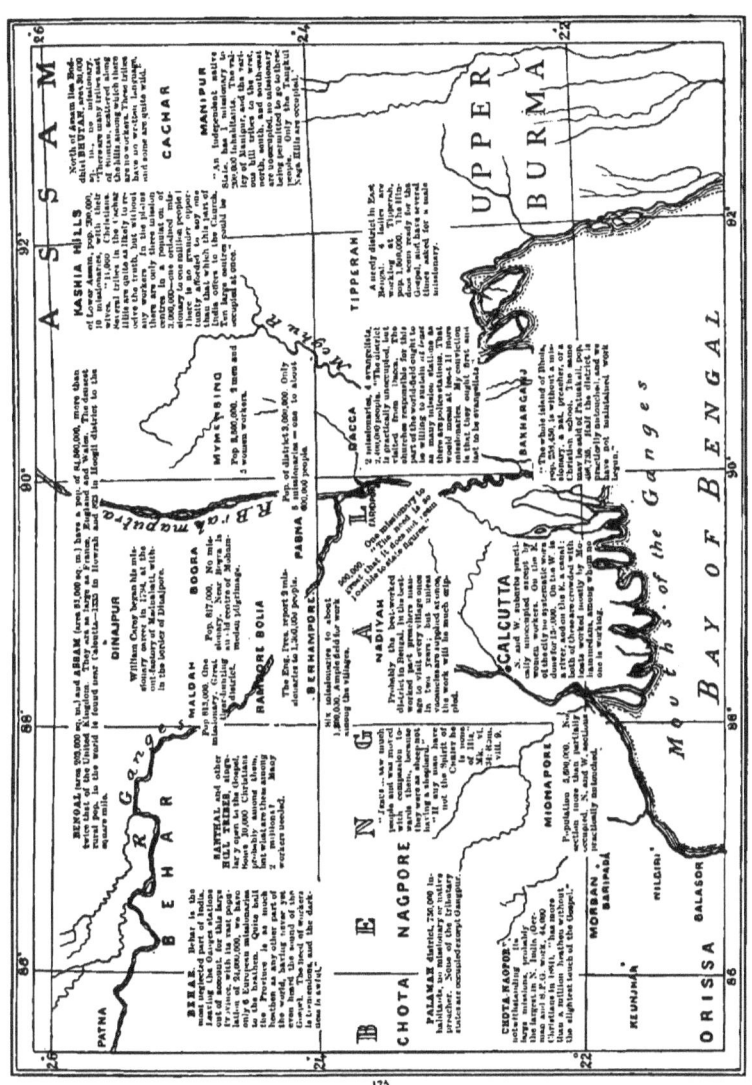

two and a half millions. South-west of Calcutta lies the crowded section Mindapur, practically untouched in the north and West, the best worked centres scarcely occupied. Nadiyah, north of Calcutta, is the best evangelised district in Bengal, 'preachers manage to visit its villages once in two years.' That is all. But Nadiyah is well off. Faridpore, lying by it, has on an average only one missionary to 500,000; Berhampore to the north again has six workers among one and a quarter millions; Rampore Bolia, north of this, only two to reach the same vast multitude; Mymensing, north-east of this among three and a half millions, has two men and five women to make known Jesus Christ.

While you think of these things the human flood sweeps on, sad faces, weary faces, faces seamed and scarred by sin, faces on which the Light of the world has never fallen. No, these here in Calcutta may have heard that God has loved us, that He is not a devourer, a god of ghouls and vampires, but Calcutta with its million men and women is so small. Behar, the opium-growing country of Bengal—a country almost as large as England, and with almost as many people—has, outside the sphere of the good work done along the line of the Ganges, twenty million people and — how can I write the words? — but six Christian missionaries, three of whom are women.

Six Christian preachers! *Six*. To twenty million people. As if in the whole of England there were six or seven ministers —no more.

* * * * *

Once William Carey stood here—the first English missionary to India. Those he had left behind at home felt that he had disappeared for ever. He never returned to England. For forty years he laboured here, and died.

'I never yet repented,' he wrote, 'of any sacrifice which I have made for the Gospel, but find that consolation which comes from God alone.' 'I have God . . . God's cause will triumph.'

ANY SACRIFICE . . FOR GOD'

To that cause he gave his all. 'To be devoted like a sacrifice to holy uses,' he wrote, 'is the great business of a Christian.' 'A Christian minister in a peculiar sense is *not his own*: he is the servant of God, and ought to be wholly devoted to Him.' . . . 'I am not my own, nor would I choose for myself. Let God employ me where He thinks fit.'

It was this spirit that brought William Carey here. It is this spirit that will bring you, too, *to the greatest need.*

BEHAR is waiting for you—half of its twenty-four millions have never heard of the love of Christ. CHOTA NAGPORE is waiting in Southern Bengal — PALAMAN, one of its districts

WILLIAM CAREY, THE FATHER OF MODERN MISSIONS.

Born 1761, died 1834. He wrote his *Enquiry* at 25 years of age; landed in Calcutta at 32, and never returned to England. In 40 years he and his companions translated the Bible, in whole or in part, into 24 Indian languages and dialects, rendering the Word of God for the first time accessible to more than 300 millions of mankind. His address at Nottingham in 1792—from which the Baptist Missionary Society arose—was based on his memorable summary of Isaiah liv. 2, 3.

'ATTEMPT GREAT THINGS FOR GOD, EXPECT GREAT THINGS FROM GOD.'

with 750,000 people, has no witness for Jesus Christ. None of its tributary States, with the exception of Gangpur, are occupied. 'More than a million heathen here are without the slightest touch of the Gospel.'

BOGRA is waiting with 817,000 and no missionary. MALDAH, the next great district, between the Ganges and the Brahmapootra river, is waiting with 815,000 souls, and but one foreign worker. If His people were really yielded to the hands of the great Master, can we suppose these vast spheres would be left uncared for?

Pause for a moment and look them out on the map. BOGRA has 30,000 more people than all Northumberland and Monmouth. MALDAH could people Bedfordshire, Cornwall, Herefordshire, and Hertfordshire, and have 4,000 over.

Beyond the teeming Ganges Delta, malarious and low, lies the beautiful hill country of ASSAM—the Kashia Hills, the Naga Hills, Hill Tipperah, and the rest. In the plains among them there are only three mission centres among three million souls. The CACHAR HILLS have as yet no workers. The valley of MANIPUR, in Lower Assam, with its hill tribes north, south, west, and south-east, is still unoccupied.

*　　*　　*　　*　　*

We are standing at the gateway. The human flood flows by—young faces, tired faces, anxious faces. Hard worldly eyes look into ours curiously and pass. What plans are seething in those busy brains! What destinies are shaping for evil and for good here in a myriad lives! And beyond, in the lives we have just thought of——

Listen. Watch. The stream flows on. Not one soul among them that thinks of God aright.

'No Bible, no Sabbaths; no house of God; no God but a log of wood or a monkey, no Saviour but the Ganges; no worship but that paid to abominable idols, and that connected with dances, songs, and unutterable impurities . . . a corrupt, rapid torrent, poisoning the soul and carrying it down to perdition. No morality, for how should a people be moral whose gods are monsters of vice;

whose priests are their ringleaders in crime ; whose scriptures encourage pride, impurity, falsehood, revenge, and murder ; whose worship is connected with indescribable abominations, and whose heaven is a——'[10]

We cannot print the words. You may read them for yourselves in any book on India's religions—words that would stain our page.

How shall these darkened millions be brought into the light? The power of God that took up William Carey, and through his and his co-workers' lives, to mention one result alone, put the Bible within reach of one-fifth of mankind, by translations accomplished in 40 years, into 24 Indian and other languages; the power of God that from the Church behind us sent Judson to Burmah, and has since raised up through that single Baptist effort 25 stations, 600 outstations, 640 churches, and some 36,000 converts in that land; and across the water, in Madras, 235 mission stations and outstations, 108 churches, and 54,000 converts from the Telugu country only, not to speak of other fields; that power is ours to-day. Why should not blessing like this come through your life to India? Why not? It did not come from Judson or from Carey. It came from Jesus Christ.

It is He who looks with pity upon this heathen world. It is He who stands beside you, facing these multitudes. As of old He says, 'I have compassion.' As of old He bids you help them. You have put your hand in the hand of Christ, and you cannot take it back.

Chapter XVII
DARJEELING

On the 26th of Feb., 1891, the British Government caused the census of India to be taken, and in less than twenty-four hours, in fact in about twelve hours, its 287,000,000 of people were all enrolled. What a testimony to the power of organised effort! How long do you think it would take to reach every soul with the Gospel if the people of God were to make it the foremost business of their lives?—DR. A. J. GORDON.

CAN you fancy what it is to be on the borders of the Chinese Empire, on the threshold of Thibet, the wall of the Himalayas stretching, white and wonderful, between you and that hidden country, but its peoples around you every day? In such a case are we! Father sits reading Gordon's life by the cheery fire in our wee room, and outside, instead of the sun-glare that almost invariably has been with us during the last ten weeks, lies a white mist veiling hills and mountains.

Five o'clock is striking from the clock in the white church on the hill, and up the steep zig-zag paths that climb from the bazaar

'THE SIMPLE PEOPLE IN THEIR GAY-COLOURED CHINESE-LOOKING CLOTHES.'

at the foot of this charming little town, come slowing toiling, like a long string of pack animals, the simple mountain people in their gay-coloured Chinese-looking clothes, loaded with heavy triangular baskets (which they carry on their backs

A CORNER OF THE BAZAAR.

by a strap over their heads), full of wares and market purchases. They are such dear creatures! I feel I love them all, and could gladly spend my life in work among them. Sturdy, healthy, cheerful, they seem a contrast in almost every way to the enervated people of the plains, and one's heart goes out to them. Their faith too seems more simple and pathetic than the repulsive Indian heathenisms. This Chinese borderland is Buddhist and demon worshipping, but not visibly idolatrous—at least no ugly idol figures mar the streets. As Father writes:—

'The mighty Himalayas have formed the material barrier by which the northward spread of Hinduism has been arrested. After a thousand years of conflict, Brahminism succeeded in expelling Buddhism from India, but it was powerless to dislodge it from the mountains and plateaux of the north. The sea of Brahminism rolled over the plain of Bengal, and covered the Deccan, but at the base of the Himalayas its advance was arrested. Here on these rocky heights, and from these mountains all across Thibet, Mongolia, and China, Buddhism is the supreme religion. The

'HIM WHOM YE IGNORANTLY

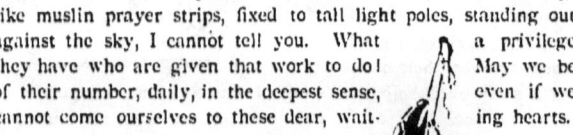

BUDDHIST
PRAYER-WHEEL.

statue of Buddha sits in imperturbable calm in ten thousand temples, and the prayer, if it be a prayer, *Om mani padmi hum*, is repeated daily and hourly with wearisome sameness by worshipping millions.'

They don't know what it means. '*O the jewel in the lotus! Hum!*' is about the most likely translation of this formula which has been used for ages, and which, written on slips of paper to be endlessly twisted round in prayer-wheels, or tied to shrubs and trees and flutter in the wind, still survives as their only form of appeal to an unknown God.

'Him whom ye ignorantly worship declare I unto you.' How those words came to my heart as I saw for the first time the flag-like muslin prayer strips, fixed to tall light poles, standing out against the sky, I cannot tell you. What a privilege they have who are given that work to do! May we be of their number, daily, in the deepest sense, even if we cannot come ourselves to these dear, waiting hearts.

*   *   *

PRAYER FLAGS
FROM
OBSERVATORY HILL,
DARJEELING.

SUCH a climb—the twenty-four hours' journey up here from Calcutta! And, as you can fancy, at 6,000 feet above sea level (as high as the Engadine) we find the weather painfully cold. The railway journey up from the plains, winding among the lower spurs of the Himalayas, is a triumph of engineering skill, and from the artistic standpoint an unbroken feast. How often in the serpentine curving of the line one could have shaken hands with the guard in the van, I should be afraid to say!

Once here you are within sight of Everest. We have just been to see him, the monarch of the snows. Starting at 4 o'clock a.m., carried by Lepcha bearers—dear, willing, sturdy creatures, not tall, but extraordinarily strong—we swung up the steep hill paths, in moonlight and starlight, under thick forest trees, past little sleeping villages, where no one moved but we, the windows dark, streets empty, our bearers imitating the cock-crow to startle the dreamers. Down into deep valleys grey with mist, then up above the frost line—up and up, till you think the bearers must give out, the gradient is so sharp—we breasted the 7,000 feet of Tiger Hill. The men breathe hard and lengthen their step, and now and then knit their brows a little; but as you study their Thibetan-looking faces in the dawn light, you

A DANDY

can see no other sign of
stress. Up and still up, the
hardy, cheerful creatures go,
now and then throwing out
a joke that sends a smile
round the calm, grave faces;
and swinging steadily on
through the rising light, till
at last you see the rose flush
on the clouds overhead, and
heartlessly urge them faster
up the last curves of the road.

THE LOOP ON THE DARJEELING RAILWAY.
(*Photographed by* Messrs. Bourne & Shepherd, *Calcutta.*)

Senchal, the great wild mountain we have climbed, lies below
us. We are pressing up the last half-mile. Weird, ruined pillars
standing out against the sky are the only sign of human habitation, besides a solitary dak bungalow. Barracks used to be here,
but the place was so lonely that the men committed suicide. Case
after case of the kind occurred, till the buildings were abandoned,
and these black rows of old chimneys are all that remain in
memory of the lives so sadly ended here. The thought of them

SUNRISE AMONG THE HIMALAYAS.

A HIMALAYAN SUNRISE

'LIKE SOME CELESTIAL COUNTRY.'

strikes colder than the chilly mountain air. But suddenly we forget them, when at a turn in the path, away across the valley and across a hundred valleys as far as one can tell, for everything between is hidden in a grey sea of cloud, we catch sight of the mighty summits of the Himalayas, shining in the dawn light like some celestial country high above this lower world of human life and pain.

What words can paint the solemnity and grandeur, purity and loveliness of their eternal snow? You know the vision of it, and the feeling that it brings to watch the change from rose to gold and then to dazzling white, as the sun climbs and day grows wide around you.

Shining above the cloud sea, 120 miles away—Everest, was it there? Once or twice we thought we saw it, three points of tooth-projecting white, and a darker rocky outline, beyond the nearer ranges, through and above the mist.

Oh, the white wall, beyond which lies Thibet! . . . To see it, not to enter, to know we cannot enter, but to know that some shall enter, and take that land for Christ!

Even now some have entered. That strong courageous woman, Annie Taylor, is there across the border as I write. Two mis-

MISS ANNIE TAYLOR IN HER THIBETAN DRESS.

sionary women are with her, and these three brave creatures, dressing in native style, and living on native food in native houses, are just beyond the pass above Darjeeling—the first stage into Thibet —17,000 feet high, keeping a little shop as a means of getting a foothold in the country. Imagine those three women, alone, without any man to protect or help them, actually at this moment in the forbidden country, teaching and preaching and circulating Scriptures! People here say that for courage Annie Taylor is equal to a Livingstone or Stanley. She seems indeed a chosen instrument, fitted to her task. God send through them His greater sunrise over the mountain wall!

Besides this young Thibetan Pioneer Mission, there are here in the Darjeeling district three missions—the Church of Scotland, with stations at Darjeeling and Kalimpong; the new Scotch 'Faith

FIRST!' 187

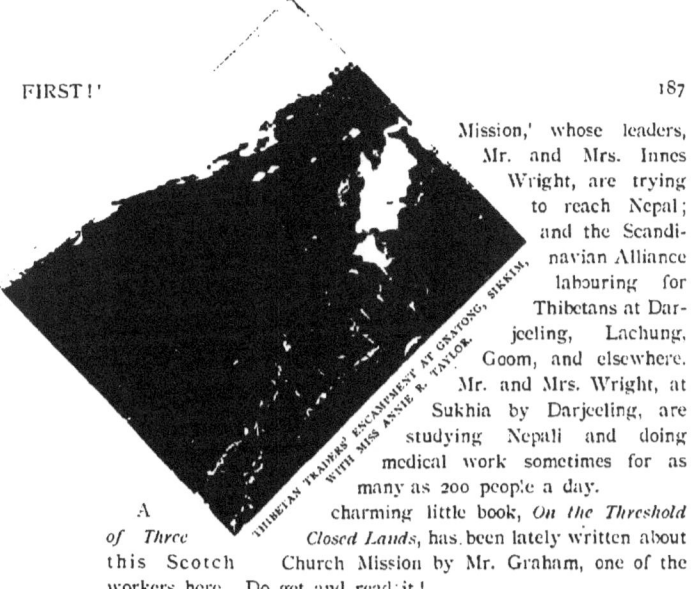

TIBETAN TRADERS' ESCAMPMENT AT GNATONG, SIKKIM, WITH MISS ANNIE R. TAYLOR.

Mission,' whose leaders, Mr. and Mrs. Innes Wright, are trying to reach Nepal; and the Scandinavian Alliance labouring for Thibetans at Darjeeling, Lachung, Goom, and elsewhere. Mr. and Mrs. Wright, at Sukhia by Darjeeling, are studying Nepali and doing medical work sometimes for as many as 200 people a day.

A charming little book, *On the Threshold of Three Closed Lands*, has been lately written about this Scotch Church Mission by Mr. Graham, one of the workers here. Do get and read it!

Their well-organised work here includes twenty schools, colportage, medical mission, a training institute for native evangelists, and over 1,800 baptised Christians.

As to the need for such effort—'The other day,' says Mr. Wright, 'at the bazaar meeting, when one of us was speaking of Christ as the only way to God and heaven, a Nepali man in the crowd, looking up at the speaker, suddenly said, "We are poor ignorant people. We do not know the true way!"'

But He who is 'the Way' is very near them; is in His servants here to lead them Home.

Chapter XVIII
BETWEEN FOUR HEATHENDOMS

Is it time for you, O ye, to dwell in your cieled houses, and this house lie waste?—HAGGAI.

UNDER 'the roof of the world,' amid its tossing land-storm, caught and fixed in mighty hills and valleys, I am sitting on the summit of Observatory Hill, with Darjeeling's pretty scattered homes at my feet.

It is early morning, fresh and cold. The market place is waking, the medley of its noises comes drifting up with the hammering of house-builders near by. The busy mountain people are already at their tasks—women and little children carrying, like the men, heavy loads of stone, wood, grain, and what not, up the steep hill paths—patient toiling beasts of burden who, with their high cheek bones, narrow dark eyes, yellow skin, lank hair hanging in long plaits, and short, thick-set figures, remind one irresistibly of China.

North of us a sea of cloud covers the whole of Sikkim, and beyond and above rise the everlasting snows, half hidden by a shifting delicate cloud veil; visible, then vanishing, till the grey screen breaks again and the majesty of Kinchinjanga flashes through, across fifty miles of country, as if it were close by.

Here on the hill-top lies a lonely tomb, the grave of some

THE KINCHINJANGA RANGE, SEEN FROM DARJEELING.

Buddhist devotee, who sought the mountains to escape the world. But what arrests one's thought is not the rough white shrine later generations have made of his resting-place, not the picturesque little town at our feet, not even the wonder of the mountains; it is the mute plea of hundreds of little paper prayer flags hanging in festoons from tree to tree, the thought that this fluttering silent appeal to the Unseen rises from countless hilltops stretching away, away—north throughout beautiful Sikkim hidden below this sea of mist, away beyond the shining wall of the Himalayas, past lonely Buddhist monasteries among the mountains, past villages and heathen shrines and scattered hamlets, on into Thibet and across that lonely tableland of 652,000 square miles, as large as Austria, Hungary, Germany, and France, and with seven million souls.

It is as if a blinded nation were reaching out helpless hands.

'OM MANI PADMI HUM'

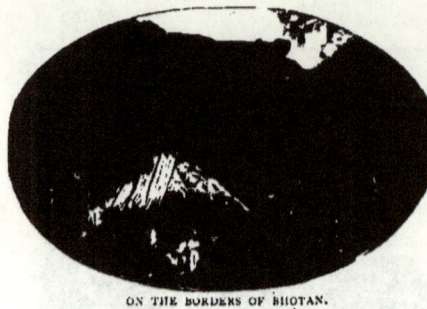

ON THE BORDERS OF BHOTAN.

The silence of these tokens of the heart's profoundest need seems a pathetic cry.

The sun is rising in the east over Bhotan. How many hill-tops there are crowned by just such prayer rags, millions of pointed bits of blue, red, green, and yellow, put up to please malignant spirits, millions of small white pennants with prayers printed on them in Chinese character. Think of that Bhotan country, lying there close beside us, wholly uncentered for Christ.

West we look towards Nepal, veiled, too, in the shrouding mist, but lying there—houses, towns, three million mountain people—Nepal, that lovely valley at the foot of the Himalayas—Nepal, still uncentered by the gospel.

When we are far away from here, busy, forgetting, working, sleeping, this mute appeal is going up to the unanswering sky. Always these silent Buddhist graves are here among the mountains, records of lives spent in this darkness, and gone beyond our reach.

Below us, to the right, in the rough Bhotia village, stands a little Buddhist temple, a common-looking native house, its single shabby inside room decked round with paintings black with age and unintelligible, its three tawdry idols hidden behind a glass, and half invisible in the darkness, its shelves of Buddhist Scriptures thick with dust, its prayer-wheels slowly grinding round '*Om mani padmi hum.*'

Again in thought we stand upon the threshold watching the lined, dull, hopeless face of the priest as with a sweep of his hand he sets a row of

'WATCHING THE DULL, HOPELESS FACE OF THE PRIEST.'

BUDDHIST TEMPLE AND LAMAS, DARJEELING.
From a Photograph] [*By* Harrison & Co., Calcutta.

prayer-wheels, each about a foot in height, spinning like teetotums. In the entry stands a heavy chest-like wheel, six or eight feet high, with two iron projections, which ring a bell each time it turns. The pleasant old wheel-turner sets it in motion with an indifferent face, chanting as it slowly revolves. We glance into the dark interior, and back at the monotonous grinding of the great wheel with its bell, and the sing-song mechanical functions of the priest. A sense of the poverty and blindness of the faith these represent comes over us, and we think what it means that just such temples are the only houses of prayer to be found throughout Thibet, Bhotan, and Nepal.

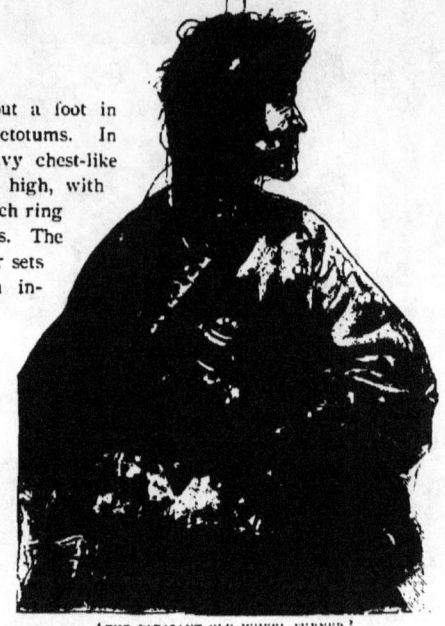

'THE PLEASANT OLD WHEEL-TURNER.'

Back to the mind come suddenly the words we read this morning, 'His feet shall stand . . . upon the Mount of Olives . . . and it shall be in that day that living waters shall go out from Jerusalem, half of them east . . . half of them west.'

His feet? Do they stand in our lives? Do they send forth living waters, east and west? Have those rivers of blessing come, through us, here?

Never, never.

But do the feet of Christ then really stand, really walk in our

lives? What were those feet? How did they walk? . . .
Oh, that life without earthly claim or possessions, that poured-
out, emptied life, spent and spent out for all the world! Is it
indeed in us?

* * * * *

The morning sun falls brightly on Darjeeling hill-tops, lighting
up the charred embers of sacred fires long ago burnt out; lighting
up the bent poles with their swaying festoons, the fallen prayer-
rags decaying on the ground among dead leaves and rubbish.
A quiet wind stirs them, softly, silently. Our time has gone.
We must go down the hill and leave this lonely summit—down
to the bazaar so thronged this Sunday morning by Nepalese,
Thibetans, Lepchas, hardy mountaineers mingling in a picturesque
throng with men from the plains, Hindus, and Europeans.

Far, far below lies India, veiled, too, beyond the clouds. We
think of it as for one last still moment we linger before leaving.

Can we ever forget this spot, this moment, the mute appeal in
the midst of which we stand? Between four heathendoms—
Thibet, beyond these northern Himalayas; Nepal and Bhotan,
west and east; India south, at our feet—between four heathendoms, and three of them unreached.

* * * * *

O JESU, O our Master, make Thou this silence speak.

From *Harper's Magazine*.   Copyright, 1895, by Harper & Brothers.
FESTIVAL OF KALI AT BENARES.

'On this occasion a very considerable portion of the inhabitants of the city spend the night on the river in large boats. Singing and dancing go on for hours. The scene is exceedingly picturesque, and its effect heightened by brilliant lights on the large boats, which are not only decorated with canopies of all colours, and lit with coloured lamps, but also crowded with passengers arrayed in fleecy garments of every conceivable hue. The boats are gaily painted. The one here shown in the foreground belongs to the Maharaja of Benares, and is decorated with the figure of a peacock gaudily painted in brilliant colours. This is the boat usually lent by the Maharaja to European visitors. The festival is in honour of Kali or Durga, the goddess of the infamous Thugs—her chief temple in Benares is known as the Monkey Temple.'

Rev. Arthur Parker, L.M.S. Missionary at Benares, author of *Handbook of Benares*—see also *The Sacred City of the Hindus* (p. 228)—the best authority on Benares.

Chapter XIX

THE FOCUS OF HEATHENISM IN INDIA

It was commonly believed that half a million of human beings crowded into that labyrinth of lofty alleys, rich with shrines, and minarets, and balconies, and carved oriels, to which the sacred apes clung by hundreds. The traveller could scarcely make his way through the press of holy mendicants and not less holy bulls. The broad and stately flights of steps which descended from these swarming haunts to the bathing-places along the Ganges were worn every day by the footsteps of an innumerable multitude of worshippers.—MACAULAY.

MIDDAY at a little wayside station, where the ticket collector at the doorway wears odd gowns. We sit together, Father and I, on the hot platform waiting for our train, with the Ganges flowing close by and a group of natives squatting on the ground in front of us. We have just come up from the river, where we have rowed along the sacred ghâts fronting the wide, grey-blue stream, passing such sights——

No, it is no use.

I feel hopeless of ever telling you what an impression the spectacle of this 'sacred city' leaves in the heart. One feels bewildered as one comes away. It seems a dream. You cannot think you have seen what you have seen.

But this sketch of Hinduism's Holy of Holies, written yesterday by Father, will give you a glimpse of India's amazing sanctuary.

*   *   *   *   *

MOSQUE OF AURANGZEB, BENARES.

PHANTASMAGORIA—such it seems, a strange incredible dream—yet is it a reality. Benares! This is India, this is heathenism.

In the golden light of the morning sun flows the broad Ganges, past the crowded flights of steps, extending mile after mile along the bank, covered with worshipping thousands, men, women, children, in white or coloured costumes or no costumes, undressing, dressing, washing, chatting, praying, pouring the sacred water on their bodies, plunging their bodies into the sacred spring,

THE BURNING GHATS

washing their hands in it, their feet, their legs, their arms their chests, their faces, their clothes; their wet garments clinging to their bodies, the water streaming off their limbs, their prayers babbling from their lips, washing away, as they imagine, both the filth of the flesh and the sin of the spirit in the self-same holy Ganges, the ever-flowing river of salvation.

The ill-savoured drainage of the city pours into the sacred stream, issuing black and fetid from wide openings on the banks, and mingling with the waters of the river. The corpse floats by, swollen and bloated, face down or face up, in the mighty flood; the vultures sit on neighbouring walls of shrines and temples, or wheel on lazy wing above the wave or light

THE GHATS: LOOKING NORTH.

upon the floating or stranded dead. Side by side on the shore burn the funeral pyres, great piles of wood blazing and smoking around newly-brought corpses, the feet of the dead protruding from the crackling flames, crowds gazing without concern on the daily spectacle. Hundreds of Brahmins sit or stand in ceremonial worship on wooden rafts built out from the stone steps on which the people of the city, or the pilgrims from distant places, are performing their religious ablutions. Suniassis, Yogis or *fakirs*, smeared with mud, giving a hideous ashen colour to their faces and bodies, with dishevelled locks, gaunt limbs, stiff attitudes, and demoniac aspect, sit on raised platforms and gaze at you, or stared into emptiness, or worship the stream, or grasp the offerings flung to them by the admiring crowd.

Above on the river banks rise the walls, the sculptures, the terraces, the towers, the pinnacles of countless temples, some dark with age, others glaring with colour, or glittering with gilded roof and spire against the clear blue sky; while beyond the shrines which line the river bank stretch the roofs of houses, closely packed together in maze-like masses whose narrow winding streets are filled with swarming thousands, struggling in the crossings, crowding round the shrines, jammed in gateways, or courts of temples, pouring water on the idols, scattering flowers on them, muttering prayers, chattering or shouting in half a score of tongues, beggars adding to the Babel by imploring *backsheesh* from every passer-by, while rich and poor cast food or money at the feet of proud and lazy priests, squatting half naked beside their senseless and abominable idols—idols in many cases too indecent for description, foul objects on which the priest publicly pours the consecrated libation, or the devotee hangs the garland or flings the flower as to a god.

O India! thy darkness is not the darkness of mere ignorance, but the darkness of lies, fantastic lies, foul lies, leprous lies, diabolical lies; thy shame is public, it is thy song and thy boast; thy gods are grovelling, bestial; with swollen bellies, black faces, elephant snouts, and protruding tongues, they glower on their worshippers from filthy shrines; their name is legion, their legends nfamous and monstrous; thy deities are demons, and thy Pantheon a Pandemonium, where millions made in the image of God prostrate themselves before beasts and devils as though they were divine. And this is thy daily habit and thy delight, this has been thy way for ages; never hast thou known the light of revelation; truth has never been truth to thee; from time immemorial things have been inverted, falsehood has been to thee truth, and truth falsehood. Who shall break thy adamantine chains? Who shall deliver thee from thy delusions? Who shall bring thee forth from thy dark prison-house, from thy horrid chambers of imagery, from thy grovelling pit of

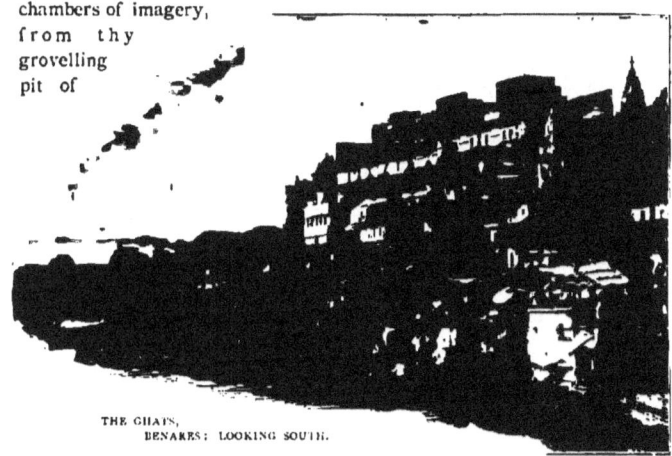

THE GHATS, BENARES: LOOKING SOUTH.

perdition into the sunlight of reality, the fair open day of truth and righteousness?

Oh, pitiable spectacle! Look at those women, grave, earnest, elderly women, walking in procession round and round that dusty old tree by the wayside, which they are taught to hold sacred, reverently sprinkling it from the Ganges, each carrying a pot of water in her left hand and a brazen-spoon in her right. Round and round they go with weary feet, sprinkling and still sprinkling as sacred the gnarled trunk and knotted roots of an unsightly tree! And this in the name of religion!

From *Harper's Magazine.*   Copyright, 1895, by Harper & Brothers.
A FAKIR, BENARES.

The fakir, riding on a sacred cow, passes, loudly demanding alms; while, sitting under his umbrella by the wayside, the *pundit* reads to the passer-by out of some old Sanscrit book words which the common people cannot comprehend. The language in which he reads has long since ceased to be spoken; it is a dead tongue; and this is all they have by way of spiritual instruction. No voice that we could hear was lifted up to protest against idolatry, or to point to the way of righteousness and salvation. And this, while Christendom crowds her cities with places of worship, and her pulpits with preachers, scatters her religious books and tracts among her favoured children by millions; fights over petty parish rights and local privileges; oblivious of great world needs, and of the state of the outlying, untaught millions of the race.

Say not 'there are missionaries in India.' There are, but what are the missionaries there to the needs?

Who shall waken the Christian Church to her duty? Look, O ye favoured ones, on the people of India; they are real men and women, with bodies and spirits, with hearts and consciences, with sins and sorrows like your own. But unlike you they are living and dying thus as we describe, without the knowledge of God, and without the knowledge of salvation. Who will come in a Christ-like spirit to their help? Who will bring them the message of the Gospel, which Christ commanded His disciples to proclaim to every creature of mankind?

THE GOSAIN TEMPLE, BENARES.

Chapter XX
WITHIN FOUR WALLS

'There are many Hindu sects in India, but upon two main points we all agree—the sanctity of the cow and the depravity of woman.'—*Hindu Saying.*

What is the chief gate to hell?
'*A.* A woman.
'*Q.* What bewitches like wine?
'*A.* A woman.
'*Q.* Who is the wisest of the wise?
'*A.* He who has not been deceived by woman, who may be compared to malignant fiends.
'*Q.* What are fetters to men?
'*A.* Women.
'*Q.* What is that which cannot be trusted?
'*A.* A woman.
'*Q.* What poison is that which appears like nectar?
'*A.* A woman.'

So runs an Indian catechism on moral subjects written by a Hindu gentleman of high literary reputation. Such are the views that paganism has made possible.

'Women,' says an Indian proverb, 'is a great whirlpool of suspicion, a dwelling-place of vices, full of deceits, a hindrance in the way of heaven, the gate of hell.'

'Never put your trust in women,' says another. 'Women's counsel leads to destruction.'

'Hear now the duties of woman,' writes the Indian lawgiver Manu. 'By a girl, by a young woman, or even by an aged one, nothing must be done independently, even in her own house. . . . Though destitute of virtue, or seeking pleasure elsewhere, or devoid of good qualities, yet a husband must be constantly worshipped by his wife.'

A WORKING WOMAN FUEL SELLER.

This, indeed, is her religion, the sum and substance of which is, as an Indian woman writes:—

'To look upon her husband as a god, to hope for salvation only through him, to be obedient to him in all things, never to covet independence, never to do anything but that which is approved by law and custom.'

With the exception of the poorest working women, whose life is necessarily unsecluded, these views find their natural outcome in the zenana system. Never shall I forget the glimpse I obtained at Benares into the working of that system; never, I think, lose the memory of the wistful eyes that followed us as we went down the stairs and out of

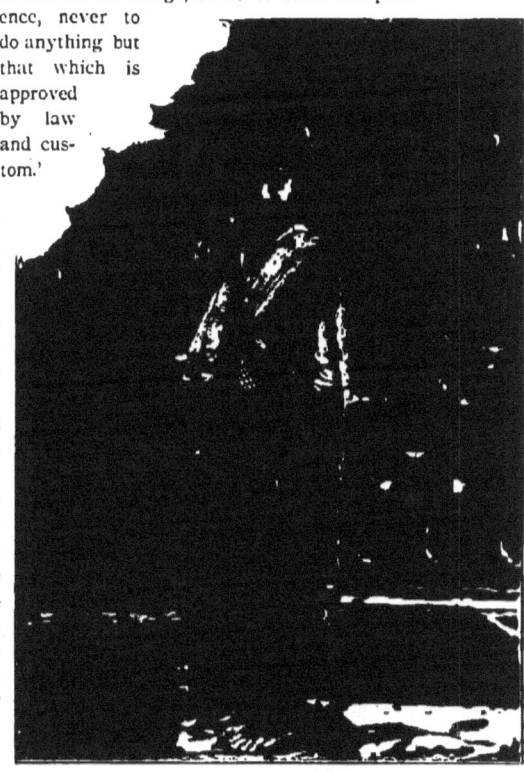

A LITTLE WORKING GIRL.
To the poorest working women life is necessarily unsecluded.

the last Hindu home I had the chance of seeing. Miss Spence, of the London Missionary Society at Benares, had taken me that morning to see some of her zenana pupils.

LOW CASTE ROPE MAKERS.

We went to several houses, all alike in principle, though richer or poorer in contents—men's apartments in front, the women's in the most secluded part of the house—mother-in-law, young wives, daughters, and children shut up within four walls.

'Do you never go out?' I asked them.

'No.'

'Would you not like to go?'

'Yes.'

'Surely you must have been sometimes?'

'Once I went down to the Ganges to bathe,' a pretty young wife told us.

'She went in *purdah*,' explained the elder woman; 'went in a shut-up *palki-gari* early, very early in the morning, before it was light. She was back before the sun rose. No one saw her.'

We looked round at the courtyard, at its mud floor and walls, its irregular doors leading into a few small rooms. The place seemed quite poor, the rooms were low and dark, almost unfurnished—no rugs or carpets, chairs or tables, pictures, sofas, ornaments—nothing but rough unpapered walls, cooking utensils, and a bed or two. Here these half-dozen women spend their lives

'GRIND AND EAT.'

—the old mother, the blind girl, the two young daughters-in-law with their children—grind and eat, bathe and sleep, sit together and gossip. The neighbours who called in to listen to the Miss Sahiba, live in just such another place next door, within four walls.

* * * *

'SHE WILL NOT SEE A MAN?'

WOMEN GRINDING CORN, INDIA.

We were waiting here for Ranee—waiting for her to dress — for her, at least, and her husband. It had been an unexpected triumph. We had called in to see her, had climbed the narrow stairs to her tiny bedroom (furnished with nothing but a bed), and had found pretty Ranee dressed in a simple half-transparent *sari*, and beaming with delight at our visit. She is the only woman in this Brahman house—a house as poor as it is proud—and spends her life in cooking and doing what small house-work is wanted in the narrow quarters she, her husband, her husband's two brothers, occupy. The father-in-law lives elsewhere usually, but is very fond of Ranee, and actually told Miss Spence one day that he would allow her to visit the Mission-house some time; but the promise was a dead letter, excuses being promptly made whenever fulfilment was proposed.

To-day, however, we pressed the husband, a slight, weak-looking creature, but devoted to his wife, whom he calls Ranee (queen) in compliment, to carry out the promise, and by dint of long persuasion have succeeded.

'She will not see a man?' he queries anxiously
'No, no; there is no man at the zenana house.'
'She must not be seen from the street?'

'You shall come with her, Kashi! You shall see her safely shut up in the carriage, and close all the windows yourself.'

'Well,' he concedes at last, after long hesitation and discussion, 'come back in fifteen minutes, and we will be prepared.'

Fifty minutes or more have passed on other visits, and now we came back to the narrow alley, in through the short passage to the hot little backyard with its ruinous mud walls, through a breach in which a bit of the next door yard is visible

'Ranee!'

A sound of shuffling upstairs. No one answers.

'Ranee!'

A pause.

Presently the husband appears on the small balcony.

'I am putting on my clothes,' he remarks.

'We have waited more than fifteen minutes, Kashi!'

'Ah, Miss Sahiba, we possess no clocks.'

Ranee's brilliant face looks smilingly over the light railing. They have both bathed and oiled themselves, and re-arranged their hair with special attention. She is dressed in delicate muslin *saris*, one over the other, each gayer than the one beneath, and daintily bordered with black. Over all she wears a soft pink *chaddah*.

After some more delay the husband comes downstairs.

'I have put on my best clothes,' he remarks affably.

It is easy to smile approval, and rather difficult not to laugh at the odd figure he presents, with his naked brown feet and legs surmounted by the usual bunch of white stuff — the *dhoti* — worn by the Hindu gentleman, plus a sky-blue shirt and European waistcoat, whose striped cloth front and cotton back are surmounted by yards of fine white muslin loosely twisted like a lady's scarf about his neck.

The anxious face of the young Brahman appears above the whole.

Copyright, 1895, Harper Brothers.

THE PALKI-GARI.
(Only the men weren't there!)

'You are sure, Miss Sahiba, that she will not see a man?'

Not till we are seated in the *palki-gari* with every shutter closed, his younger brother inside with us and Ranee, and he himself upon the box, is Kashi satisfied—if then. The jolting roads jar the carriage shutters an inch or so apart as we drive, and Ranee glances shyly out, but the brother, a lad of twelve or fourteen, hastily shuts them up. Her momentary vision of the great world is over.

How that graceful Indian woman, in her jewellery and muslins, her lips dyed scarlet with the betel she was chewing, her brilliant dark eyes flashing with delight, enjoyed that dull drive in the hot darkness of the *palki-gari*, and the few minutes allowed her in the mission-house!

The ladies dare not offer afternoon tea. To eat with us would break her caste: to suggest such a thing would be a *faux pas*. The husband is on tenterhooks lest some man should appear, and in about five minutes hurries her away back into the covered trap, and across town to the little sideway, where she lives

within four walls, cooking every morning in her tiny kitchen, waiting on her men folk, cleaning up the little house, looking forward daily to the missionary girl's visits, trying hard to learn to read, and praying for a son.

'I pray to all the gods, and now since you have come I pray to Jesus also,' she confesses.

'But the gods cannot hear you. You should pray to Jesus only.'

Ranee looks up with her soft, wistful eyes—the message is so new.

*   *   *   *   *

An elephant, almost life-size, was painted on the lower wall of the last house we went to, a large, commodious, rambling place, with half a dozen men lounging in one of the courtyards, in the midday *siesta*, and apparently no women anywhere. On a sort of lower roof, open to the hot sky, we found at last the two girls we had come to see; young, gentle-mannered creatures, who could not speak a word of English, and had not been visited much yet. We sat down on the baked-mud ruins of some old cooking places; Miss Spence brought out a primer, and the two girls pressed close to us with solemn, interested faces. Soon they were patiently attempting to spell out syllables and understand the pictures and meaning of the page—lost in a painful struggle with the mysteries of print.

The younger, a shrewd, thin child of perhaps thirteen, not married yet, strange to say, was the sharper of the two. Her companion, a placid-looking young wife, gazed with hopeless eyes upon the primer, and seemed to take in little of what was said of Christ, though she evidently liked to have us there. Puzzling out the letters, her brown finger on the page, her dark young head bent earnestly over the task, she sat in front of me, her knees pressing unconsciously against mine, her little sister-in-law equally intent beside her, making a table of my lap. We could not stay long with them; the glaring heat of the afternoon sun warned us that time was passing.

It was so hard to go—so hard to look at those young faces, with their questioning, sad eyes, seeing them thus for the first and only time, unable to express to them the blessed truth of which one's heart was full, never to see them again until that Day!

'I have hardly ever visited these girls,' said Miss Spence in explanation of their evident ignorance and anxiety to learn. 'There are so many houses! We cannot visit any of our zenanas oftener than once a week, and we cannot undertake to visit all the homes to which we are invited.'

We rose to leave. The two girls watched us, looking sad and puzzled. 'Come back soon,' said the little one.

Soon! Shall we ever go back?

We said good-bye and left them there in the women's quarters, finding our way downstairs through the rambling Hindu house till we came to the painted elephant at the entrance.

I looked back. They were standing, silhouetted against the hot Indian sky, wistfully gazing over the parapet of the roof into the inner courtyard across which we had passed. I shall never forget those faces—the dumb pleading of the eyes that followed us, the pathos of their ignorance, of their willingness to learn. Within four walls we left them waiting—waiting for Christ, for you.

Chapter XXI

IN THE NORTH-WEST

Overwhelmed by the vastness of the work contrasted with the utterly inadequate supply of workers . . . we re-echo to you the cry of the unsatisfied heart of India. With it we pass on the Master's word for the perishing multitude, '*Give ye them to eat.*' . . . Face to face with two hundred and eighty-four millions in this land, for whom in this generation you as well as we are responsible, we ask, Will you not speedily double the present number of labourers?

Will you not lend your choicest pastors to labour for a term of years among the millions who can be reached through the English tongue?

Is this too great a demand to make upon the resources of those saved by omnipotent love?—APPEAL OF THE BOMBAY DECENNIAL CONFERENCE, 1893.

BENARES! And beyond? There is no beyond for us. Thus far may we go, but no farther. We have reached our limit of time and means, and must turn our faces homeward.

With longing eyes we look across the level, sunlit country. All the historic centres seem still to lie beyond. The rose-red walls of Delhi, the ancient fort of Agra with its marble palace towers, Cawnpore with its fatal well, Lucknow where the shadow of the Mutiny still lingers, Lahore, Peshawar—all remain unseen by us. A three months' glimpse of INDIA! Everything unfinished——

We send a sigh out drifting towards the great North-West, towards the scenes still thrilling with the memories of endurance, heroism, triumph, and despair; towards the great realms of the Punjab, of Cashmere, Rajputana, Oudh, and the N. W. Frontier darkened by the cloud of war.

'Others shall sing the song,
Others shall right the wrong—
Finish what I begin,
And all I fail of win.

What matter I or they?
Mine or another's day,
So the right word be said
And life the sweeter made?'

Whittier's lines are with us as we turn away. It is not ours, that great land. 'It belongs to another man.' Yet in a sense it is ours too, and we cannot turn homeward without sweeping across it the view-glass that we have bent on India, Central, East, and West; without at least considering its spiritual needs and the spheres that from this

THE MEMORIAL WELL, CAWNPORE.

standpoint are still unoccupied in these closing days of the nineteenth century.

To do so let us travel west to the seat of war. Among the Himalayan valleys north of the Khyber Pass and the Afridi country, is the wild mountain district of KAFFIRISTAN. From its distant uplands have come to me the picture and the facts which I subjoin.

* * * * *

He had been down the steps so often, they were quite commonplace, but to-day as he came down them and turned towards his narrow room out of whose window over the little courtyard the Himalayan summits could be seen, a new idea came to him. Across the lined Siahposh face the light of a suggestion flashed.

'Why not?' he thought. 'It might end the long struggle? Why should one pour water on a "holy stone," feigning ecstasy and madness? Why offer butter, cheese, and flour to a stone? What use after all could there be in kissing and worshipping idols?'

He paused at the foot of the steps, and wondered how many times he must have sacrificed goats to the stone *Imrah Patta,* 'place of God,' and sprinkled it with their blood.

'If——' he said, and stood arrested.

Govindgar was a dreamer. As he stood there a thousand things pressed in upon his brain—the stupidity of dancing all

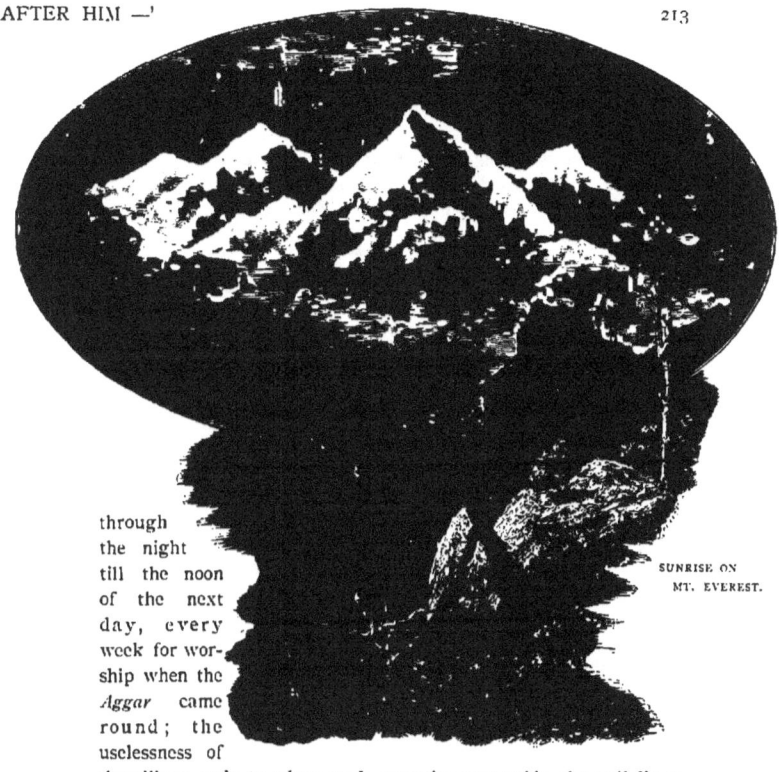

SUNRISE ON MT. EVEREST.

through the night till the noon of the next day, every week for worship when the *Aggar* came round; the uselessness of the village gods, to whom such attention was paid; the evil lives of the Moslems who urged Islam on his people; and beyond these in the grey light of a surmise he saw again the picture that had been outlined to him, of a simple childlike faith in a great Love.

Looking up, he was aware that his dull room was lighted by

a rich crimson glow. It was early. He had risen at dawn to invoke the popular idols to send much-needed rain. The sun was rising now. A tender rose tint lit the snowy summits. The majesty and sweetness of it stole through his being. It was as if the Supreme were whispering words of love.

He put out his hand blindly, and stumbled past the holy stone. For the first time he forgot his morning salutation of the household idols, and flung himself instead on the rough floor.

'*If!*'

It rang through and through him. The message had been sent. Kafiristan had invited them. If they came, the foreign preachers, if they told him the great secret whose rumour he had heard—the secret that made all life new and simple! If—if they were right? It might end the long struggle which had darkened all his life. There was no peace. He knew there was no peace. He had for ever sought it, and in vain. Yet a persistent voice within told him there must be peace, and that it could be found somewhere, somehow. If not in his own land and faith, elsewhere. And now—this he had heard of! Yes. Surely they must come?

Several weeks had passed now since the message had gone out from the little half-Thibetan village among the mountains. The peasants were discussing what the new faith could be. Was there, could there be, a god greater and better than their village idols? They would soon hear. They had sent down their message. The preachers would come now. All Kafiristan would hear.

The message travelled slowly. It filtered through by letters, and on by word of mouth. It reached its destination, and then——

The Himalayan peasants had not thought of one contingency. There was another *if*—if no one cared to answer? But that was what took place. A note about their message lies

A HIMALAYAN VILLAGE GOD.
Made of rice.

ARE NOT FED'
here upon my table, printed in a sentence in the 1896 Appeal:—

NANGA PARBAT, NEAR ASTOR, IN BALTESTAN.

'Kaffiristan some time ago asked for teachers of Christ's religion, but none have gone.'

That is all. The hearts that sent the message twenty-five years ago are waiting, and will wait.

How long, O Lord?

* * * * *

KAFFIRISTAN is a mountain country on the borders of Afghanistan. It lies due west of Cashmere, among the sublime summits of the 'roof of the world.' We have fought our way past it to CHITRAL in the north. But we left no one behind to tell of Jesus. Chitral has no missionary to-day. Kaffiristan has no preacher of the Cross.

Among the 2½ millions of Cashmere, living next door in forest and pasture lands, between great chains of snowy mountains, lie large unoccupied districts, GILGIT with its monarch peaks dwarfing Mont Blanc, PUNCH State, KISTIWAR province, ASTOR, near Nanga Parbat, far up in BALTESTAN, HUNZA, and feudatory CHILAS. A very small proportion of CASHMERE is occupied at all. The work of the good Doctors Neve of the C.M.S. is showing the love of Christ to thousands; and far away in Little Thibet or LADAK, under the unnamed peak 'K^2' of the Trigonometrical Survey, the devoted Moravian Brethren are quietly toiling on at Leh, at the still-closed gates of Thibet, ready in God's time to enter.

STREET AT SHIGAR.
BALTISTAN.

But these other gates are open. And it is we who fail. HAZARA, the most northerly district of the Indian Empire, a valley fifty-six miles wide, ' narrowing to a point in the dark gorge and still lakes of Kaghan,' HAZARA, south of Chillas, is wide open, and all but still untouched. It has 500,000 people. KOHAT, on the Upper Indus, an Afghan frontier district, south of Peshawar, with 200,000 souls, is unentered,— unattempted, while we at home are treading on each other's ground at every step, Christians among Christians evangelising Christians, over and over again.

No Christian there, no preacher, no one to reveal Christ.

PESHAWAR district is only partially occupied. All the regions north and north-west of Peshawar are unreached. One of the few workers there writes:—' The Pathans are very accessible in their villages, and hospitable. There is a great field open for itinerating missionaries. As far as I know there is no mission between this and Rawal Pindi, a hundred miles away.'

BALTISTAN, the district next to LADAK, has but one worker. You will read his appeal for help on the map. We must not tarry longer among these mountain countries. Such vast lands wait below.

Looking south from the snow-crowned Himalayas, over the Cashmere Middle Mountains, and over the bare sandstone ridges 4,000 feet in height, that spring like rugged breastworks up from the burning plains, you come to the levels of the

STREET SCENE, LAHORE, PUNJAB.

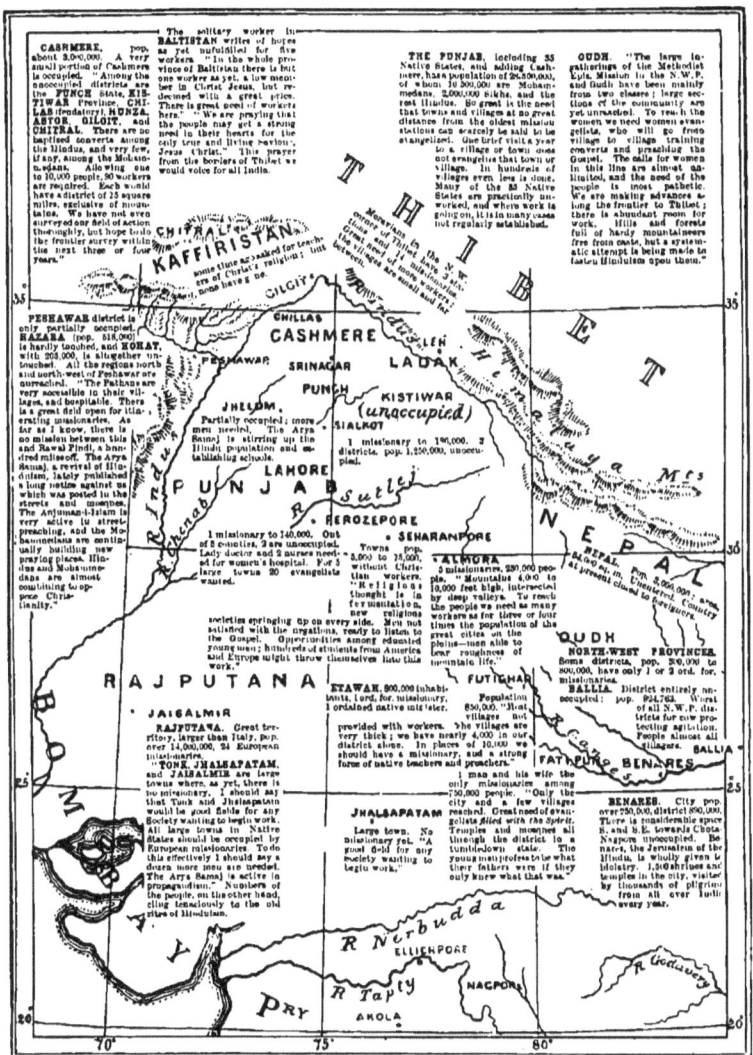

'SON, GO WORK TO-DAY

MOUNTAINS OF CASHMERE.

PUNJAB, with its five noble rivers streaming from the everlasting ice. 20,000 square miles larger than France, and with 20,000,000 people, this vast province, the largest of the twelve Provinces of India, has for ages been the highroad of invasion and war, lying at the north-western gates of India, by which successive conquerors have swept down upon the plains. Its Lieutenant-Governor controls a territory larger than the German Empire, and counts among his peoples the finest race in India—the Sikhs.

AND HE WENT NOT'

STREET IN LAHORE.

'So great is the need in the Punjaub that towns and villages at no great distance from the oldest mission stations can scarcely be said to be evangelised. . . . Many of the thirty-five Native States are practically untouched.'

Here we are in a different world to the cold high mountain country. Wide plains with crowded cities are round us. Buddhism is exchanged for Hinduism. But the one great fact of unreached heathendom remains. Districts with over a million inhabitants are waiting here. Near SIALKOTE, for instance (a well-worked mission centre), there are districts with one and a quarter million people unevangelised. Missionaries manage sometimes to visit here; but what can a brief visit do?

And this country is specially fruitful in spiritual results. Speaking of the region near Lahore, Bishop Thoburn said to me the other day —

'Had I but a score of trained men to put at once into the field, we could gather in 10,000 to 25,000 fresh converts within the next twelve months.'

But he has not got the men. And the widespread desire among some of the lower classes to turn from heathendom to Christianity is left to change or die out. There are no teachers for these people. They cannot learn of Christ.

In FEROZEPORE two counties are quite unoccupied. JHELUM district is only partly entered. But we must turn away.

'YE HAVE NOT HEARKENED UNTO

'MOVING IN DARK-SKINNED CROWDS THROUGH HOT BAZAARS.'

South of the PUNJAB lie the immense burning plains of RAJPUTANA, larger than Italy, but half desert. The fourteen million people of the Rajputana States have only twenty-four preachers of Christ.

Large towns are here—Moslem TONK (66,000, capital of Tonk State);' JAISALMIR, on a rocky ridge amid a sandy desert, an old city, founded 700 years ago the present capital of the Jaisalmir State; JHALSAPATAM, 'a good field for any Society wanting to begin work'—all without any witness to the Saviour of the world. The recent *Appeal* suggests as to Rajputana that 'all large towns in Native States should be occupied by missionaries.' It seems a modest proposal. Could one well suggest anything less?

* * * *

It is late. You will be weary. How can I write the rest? How tell about the teeming NORTH-WEST PROVINCES and OUDH—countries into which you could put the area and population of England and Wales twice over? The map on p. 217 shows them. Our hearts include them too. Districts here—but why repeat it? You can read it for yourself, printed on the map. But numbers tell so little. They do not show the people, the busy, active people moving in dark-skinned crowds through narrow streets and hot bazaars; out toiling in the country; thronging the 'sacred cities'; tramping desert sands with weary feet to reach the holy Ganges and wash away their sins. Numbers cannot show the unmet hunger of these hearts, the thraldom by which they are bound to hideous, vengeful idols; the sin in which their lives are steeped, 'without God, without hope.'

* * * * *

Has not the sad sentence of accusation, spoken 2,400 years ago, a modern application:—'*Thus saith the Lord: Ye have not hearkened unto Me in proclaiming liberty, every one to his brother, and every man to his neighbour*'?

Does it not apply to-day, to us?

'If thou forbear to deliver them that are drawn unto death——'

And how soon the chance is over! How soon our little day of life is done!

Chapter XXII
INSIDE A FAMINE POORHOUSE
'If any man have not the spirit of Christ, he is none of His.'—*Rom.* viii. 9.

BURNING sunshine falling on an acre or two of yellow sandy soil, enclosed by four long lines of sheds, roughly built, but sheltering six hundred people. Open doorless shed-fronts, famine sufferers inside: men, women, children, infants, with protruding bones, sharp shoulder-blades, sunken cheeks, and scanty clothing. Hopeless eyes sadly follow you as you pass. These people have come long distances, families together, or such remnants of them as have survived starvation.

Near the entrance you see something sitting huddled together on the ground, a creature so filthy, so old, so black, so emaciated by starvation, that the effect it presents—a small indescribable medley of skin and rags—seems scarcely human. Only, a face looks up out of it, a face hung round with matted hair, with hollow eyes and a protesting voice—'Nay, Sahib! Nay, Mem Sahib! *Nay,* Mem Sahib!'

The splendid little Englishwoman with us, a missionary of the L.M.S., who with her comrades has been here for months fighting the famine, offers to take in this wretched being; but the poor old woman—it is a woman—refuses.

'No, Mem Sahib, no.' She would rather beg here on the road, close to the town of Mirzapur; and on the road we leave her, under the scorching midday sun, probably soon to die.

Our bright, energetic guide chats kindly to the people as we pass down the long lines, everywhere meeting the same sights. Two or three native officials are standing about.

'How many deaths last night?' she asks.

'Ten, Mem Sahib.'

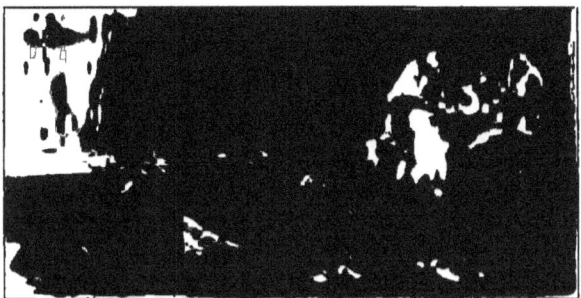

built round it. But here the suffering is worse. Many in the poor-house are merely thin and hungry-looking in spite of the rations regularly given out; here one is arrested by staggering forms too weak to stand, piteous dysentery cases, ghastly limbs with skeleton hands and feet attached to them, sufferers lying in the burning sun, the brown skin strained like parchment across the ribs, and falling beneath them into an appalling cavity one would not think could co-exist with life. The painful postures, faint coughing, pitiful appealing voices begging for food, feeble movements too weak to brush away the swarming flies, the sickening stench that meets you here and there, the low wailing cry of children with unkempt hair or shaven diseased heads, the unchildlike expression of despair on little faces that seem to have forgotten how to smile, the crouching figures trembling with weakness and pulling scanty coverings about them—these things repeat themselves around you till you ask yourself, 'Am I in hell?' and feel that death is merciful to end such suffering.

Death is not far away. Some one calls you out behind a corner shed. Your guide is standing there silent beside a body stretched like the rest upon the ground. She draws aside a little of its covering. The cheek is flat on the bare earth. The shaven skull, the bony withered breast, the emaciated limbs and stark feet projecting below the rough cloth, lie naked in the hot Indian sunshine.

Only one more famine 'case': a Hindu woman starved to death. The flies are buzzing round her. You look and turn away.

* * * * *

'It came to pass that the beggar died, and was carried by the angels into Abraham's bosom. The rich man also died, and was buried; and in hell——'

'When once—and only once—Christ lifted the veil of the world beyond, it was to reveal one tormented in the "white heat of God's indignation," whose offence was not that he was rich— Abraham was as rich as Dives, perhaps richer—his sin was in this, that he found life's good in his goods, and not in doing good; and that *he left his poor brother at his gate, unpitied, unrelieved.*'

* * * * *

Although the Government of India estimated that six millions of money would be needed to efficiently relieve the famine of 1897, not more than one million was given by England that spent ten times as much with a light heart on her Diamond Jubilee celebrations. What mockery it seems to call ourselves a Christian nation when we lavish millions without thought or hesitation for the showy spectacle of a single summer's day, and cannot afford more than a sixth of what is needed to relieve *thirty millions* of our fellow-creatures suffering from 'one of the most terrible calamities that ever afflicted mankind.'

Amid the horrors of the present starvation time, there is a group of men in India whose inhumanity presents a picture more sad to contemplate than even the condition of perishing thousands. The Indian grain-seller, or *bania*, living in close proximity to, or actually within, the famine country, looks upon the present dis-

tress as a means of making money. Finding a longed-for opportunity in the dearth and the Government policy not to interfere with trade, he hoards large quantities of grain, combines with his fellow-tradesmen—helped by the caste system—to control the market, and waits for prices to reach the highest figure before he will sell out.

Is it possible that the moral burden of such a crime as this attaches in any sense to us? The unutterable cruelty of making direct gain for oneself out of the sufferings of our fellow-creatures can never, thank God, be laid to our charge; but if there is anything—influence, help, gifts, or the power of getting gifts from others—that we might give and are not giving India, is not a parallel sin to that of this sin of the *bania* in some sense our own?

Chapter XXIII
THE RIVERS OF THE UNWATERED LAND

When the poor and needy seek water, and there is none, and their tongue faileth for thirst . . . I will open rivers in high places . . . I will make the wilderness a pool of water.

MANGO GUSOR.
(A HIMALAYAN PEAK.)

INDIA is the country of great rivers. From the snows of the Himalayas, the heights of the Western Ghauts, the mountain ranges of Aravalli, Vindhya, Bhaurer, Kaimur, and Satpura; from the Suleman uplands on the Afghan frontier and the Rajmahal hills of Bengal, from the broken line of the Eastern Ghauts and the wild passes of Cashmere, a generous flood of waters pour ceaselessly down to the sea. Over a score of rivers, each dwarfing our Thames, the smaller ones quadrupling England's greatest stream, the larger multiplying it half a dozen times in length and forty or fifty times in volume, stretch their gleaming silver lines in a vast beneficent network, carrying throughout the continent of India water enough to amply supply her 300 millions.

But what is this wealth of water doing? For the most part running to waste. We have to-day in India the extraordinary

ANICUT (OR WEIR) ACROSS THE MAIN BRANCH OF THE GODAVERY RIVER AT THE HEAD OF THE DELTA, WITH SLUICES, AND HEAD OF THE EASTERN MAIN CANAL.
Weir a mile long : canal 60 yards wide, with 8 feet of water.

fact that while one hundred cubic miles of water are swept down annually to the ocean, fifty or sixty millions—a population equal to that of the United States, or of the United Kingdom and all her colonies—are suffering from famine throughout vast areas, simply for want of water.

The Government of India has lately published a fifty years' irrigation story—the history of the Godavery Irrigation Works begun in 1846, costing £800,000, demanding a single weir 4,000 yards in length, built with 1,000,000 tons of masonry, three main canals broader than the Thames at the head of tide-water, and 2,600 yards of earth embankments linking the delta islands, to control the flood-tide of the freshes when the river (nearly four miles broad at its delta head) rises thirty feet and discharges 190,000,000 cubic yards per hour.

Fifty years ago a Commission sent to inquire into the poor condition of the Godavery district, strongly recommended the

330 BENEFICENT RESULTS

GENERAL SIR ARTHUR COTTON, R.E., K.C.S.I.

making of these works. The story of what followed, told by Sir Arthur Cotton, R.E., whose memory of India runs back seventy-five years, and includes forty-five years of Indian service, is of the deepest interest.

'It is impossible,' he writes of the irrigation labours, 'to imagine the violence of the prejudice against these works on the part of the whole body of the members of the Governments of Calcutta and Madras. But Madras had a remarkable man at that time as Governor, the Marquis of Tweeddale, who, almost alone, succeeded in persuading the India House Directors to sanction the project for the complete control of this vast river.

'The works were begun in 1846, and have been carried on from time to time almost to the present. From the very first year the remittances from the district to Madras have gone on increasing, such being the enormous results of river irrigation, that the increase of revenue from improvement and extension, even while the main head works were under execution, more than covered all the expenditure.

'The three main canals allow of eight feet of water, flowing at about 1,600,000 cubic yards per hour, the whole distributed over 700,000 acres of land, yielding an increase of produce of about 40 rupees per acre, or together 280 lacs of rupees a year, besides all the vast saving on 500 miles of first-class water transit for vessels of 250 tons, and 1,500 miles of minor canal.

'The results up to the present time are about 100 lacs a year against 20 lacs before 1846—a five-fold increase.

'The increase of population has been from half a million to two and a quarter, or four and a half fold; that of sea trade fifteen-fold.

'The increase of income to the people by the irrigation of 700,000 acres, the protection of the crops from floods by embankments and drains, the almost abolition of the cost of internal carriage by the thousands of miles of water transit, etc., cannot have been less than four or five million pounds a year—equal to three times that sum in England.

'When I tried to persuade the Secretary of State for India to set us free to carry on the works effectively by authorising an annual expenditure of five lacs of rupees a year, he said, "It's all very well for you engineers to talk in this way, but you haven't to provide the money." I replied, "I only ask for half" (I might have said a quarter) "of the increase of revenue that we ourselves have provided already, and the increase is going on more rapidly every year."

'Nothing can be more astonishing than this strange opposition to irrigation and internal navigation. The Godavery might at this moment be pouring rice into the famine districts of the North in immense quantities at a nominal cost of carriage of one penny a bushel, if only the several pieces of canal in the 1,000

miles between were united, which they might be for the cost of twenty miles of railway.'

Sir J. Lyall, formerly Lieutenant-Governor of the Punjab, has also drawn attention to facts as to the benefits conferred by irrigation on the Punjab scarcely less striking than those adduced by Sir A. Cotton.

UPPER PART OF THE MAIN WESTERN CANAL FROM THE KISTNA, WITH THE HILL ON WHICH ONE END OF THE ANICUT RESTS.
A Canal of 90 miles connects the Kistna and the Godavery.

Sir Arthur Cotton urges that all, and more than all, the revenue now gained by the Indian Government from the opium traffic with China might be obtained from irrigation works, which would, besides their yield of revenue, be a blessing instead of a curse to the population concerned, and would be the best possible safeguards against famine. But famine still sweeps away millions and India's magnificent rivers pour ceaselessly into the sea.

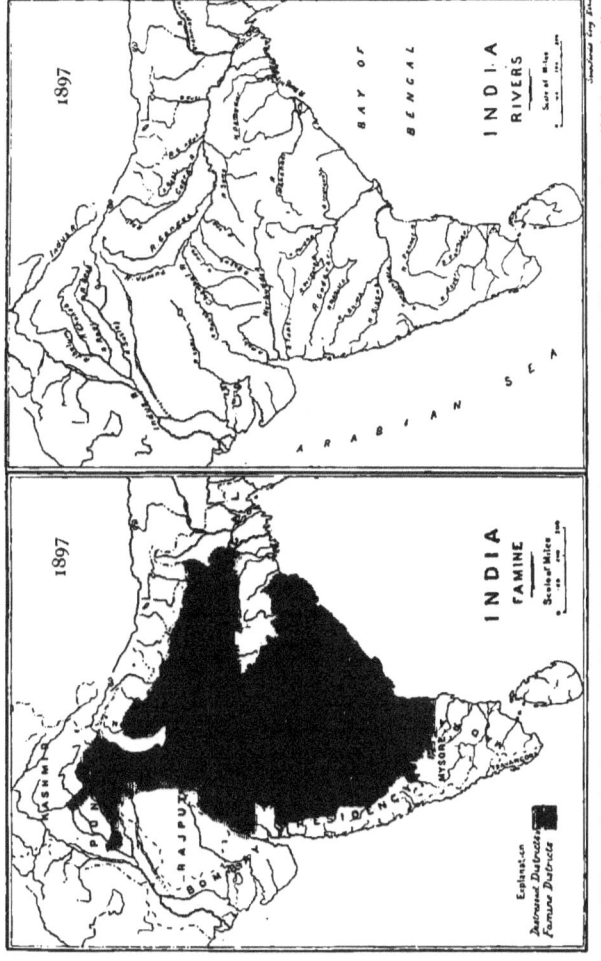

While 100 cubic miles of water are poured by the rivers of India into the ocean every year, 50 or 60 million people, scattered over half India, are reduced to distress or actual starvation by famine for want of water. The well-irrigated district of the Upper Ganges and Jumna canals will be noticed between the Punjab and the N.W. Provinces on the map.

Chapter XXIV
'RIVERS OF LIVING WATER'

I will pour water upon him that is thirsty, and floods on the dry ground. I will pour My Spirit on thy seed, and My blessing upon thine offspring. . . . Ho, every one that thirsteth, come ye to the waters. If thou knewest the gift of God . . . thou wouldest have asked of Him, and He would have given thee living water. . . . Whosoever drinketh of the water that I shall give him shall never thirst, but the water that I shall give him shall be in him a well of water springing up into everlasting life. He that believeth on Me . . . out of his body shall flow rivers of LIVING WATER.[1]

'THIS spake He of the Spirit, which they that believed on Him should receive.' And never a word of His went forth that was not true.

'Rivers of living water'? How they have sprung from the infinite Source, how they have streamed through the ages, how they have turned the desert into the garden of God!

Christianity is the religion of great rivers, the faith of floods

---

[1] Isa. xliv. 3; lv. 1. John iv. 10-14; vii. 37.

of blessing. They have been. They shall be. Even now they flow through many a life. And they may flow through ours.

JOHN WESLEY, against whom the churches were closed, driven into the open air, and there so preaching that ten to twenty or thirty thousand people would come together and wait for hours to hear; travelling, during the fifty years of his unparalleled apostolate, 250,000 miles, and preaching 40,000 sermons, besides writing and editing a library of religious and educational works—commentaries on the whole of the Old and New Testaments, a score of volumes of his own, and fifty editions of other writers, till through the popularity of his books he 'unawares became rich,' and made £30,000, every penny of which he distributed in charity during his lifetime; WESLEY, exclaiming, 'The world is my parish,' dying with the words, 'The best of all is God is with us,' and leaving behind him churches extending over Europe, America, and the West Indies, numbering 80,000 members, and since increased throughout the world to 25,000,000 — was not this man the channel of a river of water of life? WHITEFIELD, with his irresistible eloquence, and mar-

vellous voice 'capable of reaching 20,000 men on a hillside,' preaching 18,000 sermons to no less than ten millon people in his incessant widespread tours, speaking, like Wesley, in the open air when parish pulpits were denied him, and moving alike rough colliers, who would stand in listening thousands, the tears streaming down their grimy faces, and cold critics like Hume and Chesterfield—these men, not to speak of the men of our own time, through whom the same great stream of life flows on, what are they but channels of a divine 'flood'?

How have the living waters flowed far off into earth's deserts through simple human lives! WILLIAMS, among the savages of the South Seas, evangelising 300,000 of the lowest heathen, his visit to England 'thrilling tens of thousands, and doing more to fan the flame of missionary interest than any event which had occurred for a century': DUFF, twice shipwrecked on his journey out, 'cast like seaweed upon the shores of India,' saving from his library of 800 volumes nothing but his Bible and a Psalter, and with this equipment transforming the missionary body of Calcutta, whom (with the exception of Carey) he found hostile to his plans, starting Christian colleges that extend now throughout India, and swaying thousands at home with 'sublime appeals that sent them forth, not like the audiences of Cicero, saying, "What a mighty orator!" but like those of Demosthenes, exclaiming, "Let us go and fight the enemy!"' till the Scottish churches were aroused to missions with the generous enthusiasm that distinguishes them to this day: JUDSON, the father of American missions, declining the pastorate of the leading Boston Church, and going out to meet in Burma imprisonment and fetters, fever and half starvation, daily and nightly suffering for months, and hourly anticipation of death; losing his wife and little child, till, with broken heart and health, he became almost ascetic, fasting and praying whole days in the woods, and led through this baptism of pain into the founding of a Burmese Church, which numbers to-day 30,000 communicants besides a great company who have fallen asleep: ROBERT MOFFAT, toiling with his wife among low South African heathen, the people turning a deaf ear to his doctrines till he exclaimed, 'Mary, this is hard work, and no fruit yet appears!' the believing wife quietly writing home for a Communion Service with the words, 'it will be wanted'; ROBERT MOFFAT, toiling on for fifty years, translating the entire Bible into the Bechwana, journeying north among the unreached Matabele, winning the hearts of the natives to Christ, till at the opening of their Church 150 Christians sat down to the Supper of the Lord; and returning to England with his devoted wife, after fifty years of service, to move thousands of hearts by pen and lip for Africa's down-trodden races: through these lives, and such as these, has not the Word of the Master been fulfilled, 'He that believeth on Me, out of the depths of his being shall flow rivers of living water'?

What streams of love, of self-abnegation, of pity for the suffering, have flowed across the heathen world, making the deserts blossom where they ran! And what refreshment did the workers find from the exhaustless Fountain. Amid the toil and loneliness they drank of the river of God.

'I shall never taste a deeper bliss,' said Paton, of the first Aniwa Communion, 'till I see the glorified face of Jesus Himself.'

'*Gottes Brünlein hat Wassers die Fülle*,' as Luther's German has it—'God's springs are always full.'[1]

These living waters have transformed whole kingdoms. In our own time we have seen it. Only twenty-two years have passed since Stanley sent from Uganda his challenge written amid the horrors of unbroken heathenism—burning, impaling, and maiming of victims going on all round him at the king's com-

---

[1] Psalm lxv. 9.

mand. Only twenty years ago in answer to that challenge the first Uganda missionaries began the work whose story was written for the first twelve years in suffering, weakness, difficult toil, massacre, fever, travel, death; and, when the Gospel began to take effect, in mutilation and martyrdom of converts, a storm of persecution that threatened to blot out the little Church. Uganda Christians were slaughtered in horrible ways, they were placed in furnaces and slowly roasted to death, they—but we cannot tell the story here. It has been finely summarised in two brief articles in the June and July numbers of the *Missionary Review of the World* for 1897. Read it there for yourself, and note the closing figures, statistics of to-day:—

57,300 readers in 16 provinces. 321 churches accommodating 49.751. Sunday attendance, 25,300. Week-day attendance, 6,300. 725 qualified teachers. 22,972 'Mateka' readers (in elementary preparation). 20,586 'Gospel readers' preparing for Christian baptism. 35,743 New Testaments and Gospel portions sold. 6,905 baptized Christians. 2,591 Catechumens, 1,355 Communicants.

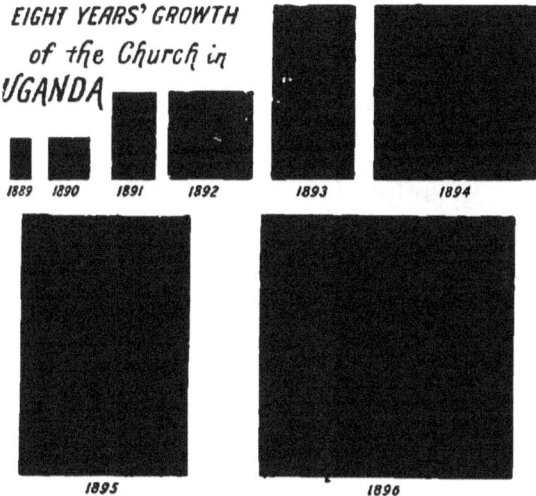

'LIKE A RIVER GLORIOUS.'

All this in twenty years and in the heart of Central Africa. What does it mean but the flood-tide of the river of water of life?

And what can we more say? Time fails to tell the story of WILLIAM BURNS in China, ELLIOT and BRAINERD among North American Indians; LIVINGSTONE, from whose grave seven Central African Missions sprang; of ALLEN GARDINER writing, 'My soul, wait thou only upon God, for my expectation is from Him,' on the rocks of the Fuegian beach, where, after nine months' abandonment, he and his companions died of hunger, the South American Mission springing from their death; of PATON in cannibal islands, winning out of vice and misery jewels for the crown of the Eternal King; of the first Congo labourers when, after years of fruitless toil, 1,200 heathen, at one station only, were swept in a single fortnight into the Kingdom of God; of the forty years of Telugu seed-sowing and the thousands there born in a day; of the long, long line of blessed workers stretching from the shining names of our own time, back to the absorbing missionary zeal of ZINZENDORF and the first Moravian pilgrims nearly 200 years ago.

Such work is never easy. What Paton felt on first seeing the South Sea heathen was probably an experience familiar to them all.

'On beholding these natives in their paint and nakedness and misery,' he wrote, 'my heart was as full of horror as of pity. Had I given up my much-beloved work and my dear people in Glasgow, with so many delightful associates, to consecrate my life to these degraded creatures? Was it possible to teach them right and wrong, to Christianise or even to civilise them?'

But by the cleansing living Stream the great transformation was effected—effected by the overflow of blessing from hearts whose thirst was quenched, and that borne on the flood-tide of the river of God could say,—

'It was no matter when, nor where, nor how Christ should send me, nor what trials He should exercise me with, if I might be prepared for His work and will. . . . All my cares, fears, and desires . . . were in my esteem of little more importance than a puff of wind. . . . I cared not where or how I lived, or what hardships I went through, so that I could but gain souls to Christ.' [17]

'The whole earth is the Lord's; men's souls are His; I am a debtor to all.

'I would rather be despised and hated for the sake of Jesus, than be beloved for my own sake. . . . I have but one passion, and it is He, He.' [18]

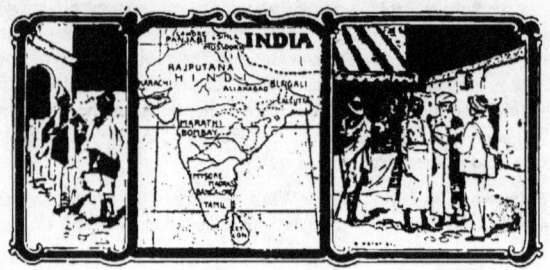

Chapter XXV

'IF——'

'Where with us is the spirit of Paul, who, when he spoke of those that were enemies of the Cross of Christ, blotted the page on which he wrote with his tears? We take it all too easily, far too easily. We see the heathen perishing, and we know they are perishing; but yet we go about our ordinary life and avocations as though there were no such thing as perishing people, and as though we could not do infinitely more than we are doing to try to save them.'—ISABELLA BIRD BISHOP

ONE of the most solemn sentences in the Bible is in Jeremiah xxiii. 22—'*If they had stood in My counsel, and had caused My people to hear My words, then they should have turned them from their evil way, and from the evil of their doings.*'

The words occur in the protest against the Jewish prophets, that fills thirty-two verses of the chapter, commencing 'My heart within Me is broken because of the prophets.' It is the protest of the heart of God, not against the wickedness of the land, but against those who possessed the means of arresting that wickedness—means given to them that they might arrest it—and did not use the power and treasure they possessed. The land was 'profane, . . . full of an horrible thing . . . as Sodom, and the inhabitants as

Gomorrah.' Yet 'Ye shall have peace,' the prophets were saying. 'No evil shall come upon you.' And all the while 'the whirlwind of the Lord,' even His grievous judgments, was about to fall upon the sinful nation.

Does the heart of the story lie in that word 'if——'?

There was a higher counsel in which they might have stood. There was an availing message that would have saved the land. It was not too late. Even then, with Assyria hanging like a storm-cloud on the frontier, and the thunder of invasion in the air, the captivity might have been averted. If——

But they did not do it. They did not cause the people to hear the word in which deliverance lay. The black storm gathered closer and broke across the land. And to the prophets' negligence God charged the people's ruin.

Has it no meaning for us? Do not we hold a message that is 'the power of God unto salvation to every one that believeth'? Do we not know—even omitting the great questions of eschatology—that the souls that are living without Jesus Christ to-day are perishing? From the heart of the Mohammedan world Robert E. Speer, one of the Secretaries of the American Presbyterian Board, writes of the immoralities of Islam—

> Under such practices it is no wonder that one sees here in the main, not the attractive women and the handsome, stalwart, active men of whom we read in books, but wrecked and weakly men and women, aged and shrivelled before their time. . . . Mohammedism has not saved woman from man. In multitudes of instances it has not saved man from his brother. . . . The opium curse and the lust authorised by the Koran are visibly eating out the life of Persia. Her manhood is rotting away.

Not Persia only.

And the bitterness and pity of it is that the modern 'prophets'—we who now hold the Word of God—have in our hands a message that can save. And that we do not give it to two-thirds of the world.

* * * * *

There is a greater famine than that of India; greater because more widespread, deeper, lasting longer, affecting human souls as well as bodies. There is a hunger covering the world, seen in a million idols, fetishes, temples, shrines; in innumerable heathen prayers, penances, offerings, gifts of money; in countless lives that seek deliverance from sin,—heathen monks, nuns, fakirs, devotees. What are these pilgrims travelling from the islands of Malaysia, from North, South and East Africa, from India, Turkey, the Soudan, Arabia, even China, drawn to that old black stone, the Mecca *Kaaba*, the heart of the Moslem world? What are these other pilgrims tramping the vast expanse of India, hundreds of thousands seeking the corrupt 'sacred cities,' foci of Hinduism? What is this endless repetition throughout the Buddhist world, of syllables without meaning, this everlasting telling of rosaries, grinding of prayer-wheels, flutter of prayer-flags?

PILGRIMS ENTERING MECCA, THE HEART OF THE MOSLEM WORLD.

There is a greater famine—hunger of men and women for the knowledge and love of God.

How is this hunger met? Let your mind return to the multitudes we thought of, living in India only—KUTCH, with as many people as Uganda, and no missionary yet; MANIPUR valley and hill tribes; BOGRA with 817,000; MALDAH with 815,000; BHOLA and PATNAKALI in Bakhargang, with 800,000 between them; NATIVE STATES in the PUNJAUB; BALLIA district with nearly a million people; three sections in SIALKOTE with 1¼ millions; large counties in MYSORE, great STATES in HYDERABAD; nearly all the NATIVE STATES of the CENTRAL PROVINCES; CONJEEVERAM, close to Madras; far away north in Cashmere, KISTIWAR Province, CHILLAS, HUNZA, ASTOR, GILGIT, CHITRAL, PUNCH; KAFFIRISTAN over the border; and finally nine-tenths of BEHAR with over 20 million people—in all these immense regions, among all their teeming villages and cities, no one to preach Christ to thirsting hearts; no one after 1,900 years of His command and of heathendom's appeal for living water . . . No one . . . no one yet.

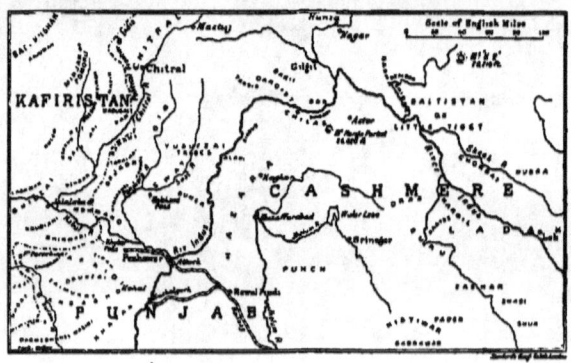

There is a greater famine. There is a greater sin. It is the old, old sin of the prophets done to-day, and done by those who bear the name of Christ.

And the bitterness and pity of the situation is that we *might* transform the world, if——, if——

We have thought of the rivers of India, but what are they compared to the rivers of living water within our reach? If we but lived nearer 'the Fountain of living waters,' if we were but utterly yielded to be His channels, the river of God would flow through us, as it flowed through the lives we have thought of, in blessing to the world. It is promised. It is certain. '*He that believeth on Me . . . out of his body shall flow rivers of living water.*' '*The works that I do shall he do also, and greater works than these*——' Greater works? Yes, the arm of God is able—the arm we move by prayer. There is a higher Counsel, a realm in which we ought to live among the thoughts and purposes, the love, the life of God. To dwell here, to make these know, must change the world.

'*If they had stood in My counsel, and caused My people to hear My words. . . . Is not My word like a fire? saith the Lord; and like a hammer that breaketh the rock in pieces?*' It is not we who can do this work. It is His availing revelation of Himself.

* * * * *

The lament rings down the ages. '*My* people!' spoken of a nation sunk in idolatry.

There is no drunkard staggering down our streets: no woman pacing them with a profaned heart and life; no opium slave yielding to the habit that enslaves him; no heathen bowing down to senseless idols; no Buddhist putting up his fluttering prayer rags, or grinding his prayer-wheel; no young man in our homelands taking the first fatal step of a ruined life; no heart-broken girl hurrying to end her shame by suicide, of whom God does not say as here, though in a different sense, 'My people!'

And more: there is no great national sin—drink and opium demoralising subject races, vices of our own people libelling Christianity, atrocities of conquering Europeans perpetrated against helpless

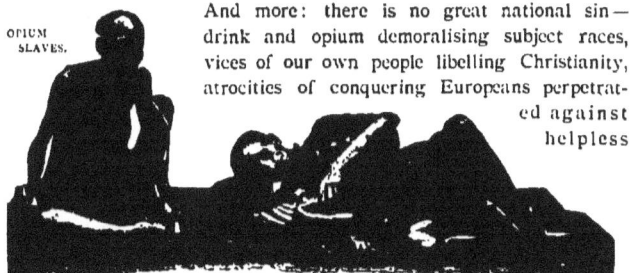

OPIUM SLAVES.

natives, war involving nations in innumerable crimes—there is no evil darkening the fair face of God's earth, for which His Church is not ultimately responsible, and which she could not sweep away if she but used God's power. 'If——'

* * * *

He came through the garden in the midnight alone. He came to seek for love, for an understanding heart. He was bearing the sorrow and sin of all the world. He had gone through the conflict in agony and blood. Even then He might have saved Himself. He might have done His own will. But He chose to bear the cross for us, and to die the death of all.

Earth's greatest strife was over, and He came to seek His loved ones. He had bid them watch and pray—share with Him the trial and the service of that hour.

Did He crave in that great moment one sympathetic heart?

He came and found them sleeping.

And so to-day He passes among these we forget; feeling the sin and sorrow, just as He used to feel them, caring as He used to care for each soul of all earth's millions alienated from the love and holiness of God. In spirit still He moves unseen among the thronging streets and populous wide districts that have not even heard His blessed name. Unseen He comes to us, to-day, seeking for hearts to share with Him the trial and the service.

'Could ye not watch with Me,' He says, 'one little hour?'

It is late. The Master listens and we make no reply. He comes to us, and finds us to the needs of half the world—still asleep.

'AND HE COMETH AND FINDETH THEM ASLEEP.' [*Sir Noel Paton.*

Chapter XXVI
CONCLUSION

I am but one, but I am one ; I cannot do everything, but I can do something ; what I can do, I ought to do ; what I ought to do, by the grace of God I will.

NO, not asleep; awaking.

He finds His Church at the dawn of the twentieth century more awake than ever before to the spiritual needs of India. He finds thousands of His people living for His kingdom there; 1,700 of them Indian missionaries; thousands of them, scattered the wide world over, giving time and money, giving sons and daughters, giving thought and love and prayer to India.

Yes, as the 19th century passes away for ever, amid war, plague, famine, earthquake, amid the shout of Jubilee, the forward march of progress, and the reaching out of the nations' hands towards His universal peace, He finds thousands of His people daily upon their knees, doing the greatest work that hearts can do for India.

From America, from Australasia, from our little British Isles, from the Continent of Europe and the bright lands of the East, He hears these daily prayers rising, rising, ever rising; importunate, continuous, believing, bound to avail.

Do you not think He is going to answer them more blessedly than any of us expect? Do you not suppose He has greater things in store to give than He has ever given—He 'who is able to do exceeding abundantly above all that we ask or think?' What will He do for India? What shall we ask Him to do? What but that His

'OUR LONG HOME.'

Church may fulfil His own commandment, may carry the news of His love and His redemption 'to every creature' there? Two-thirds of this vast India, of this Empire-realm of ours, with its huge population, knows nothing still of what CHRIST is, can be, will be, has been; has no idea that India's need was part of the reason why He came.

At the dawn of the 20th century is the Church of JESUS CHRIST to be content with what she has already done here? Is she to look forth on no wider prospect than the maintenance of her small existing work? What about these unevangelised 200 million souls? We are supporting Indian Missions? True. But none of them reach *these*. None of them reach any of the Moslem and heathen multitudes whose location and utterly neglected state is shown on the four type maps of this little book.

When you and I, if our LORD delay His coming, lie down in our 'long home,' with the work of life behind us, and our one chance of earthly service gone, when that hour—possibly so near—comes, what record will it seal for us and *these?* What shall we have done for BALLIA with its million people and no missionary? For HYDERABAD's eight or ten unevangelised millions? For the twenty millions living wholly unreached in BEHAR? What can we do to-day for these?

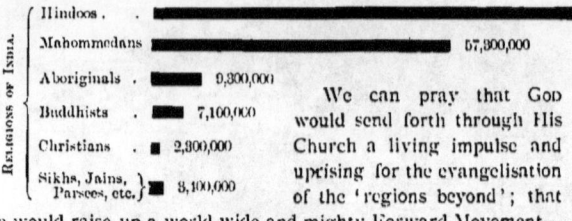

We can pray that GOD would send forth through His Church a living impulse and uprising for the evangelisation of the 'regions beyond'; that He would raise up a world-wide and mighty Forward Movement—by what instruments we know not, He will choose—to take in charge the great work which nobody is doing. Why should not every missionary speaker, every volunteer for the foreign field, every one who advocates by pen, or lip, or prayer, or effort, the evangelisation of the world, step forth across the threshold of the new century with a practical purpose expressed in a new watchword and life-aim, for an adequate

'REGIONS BEYOND FORWARD MOVEMENT'?

Why not?

It would be too great? The Church is strained already to maintain existing work? Alas, no! She is sleeping. She is not yet half awake to the duty of the task, let alone its execution. She could do it in one generation were she but aroused—yes, in this generation.

'*Bring ye all the tithes into the storehouse, that there may be meat in Mine house, and prove Me now herewith saith the Lord of hosts, if I will not open you the windows of heaven, and pour you out a blessing, that there shall not be room enough to receive it.*'

'*Open thy mouth wide and I will fill it.*'

'*Greater things than this shall ye do, because I——*'

We are standing midway in the plans of God, beset by His providence, drawing from His illimitable power. Behind us lie the ages in which the Cross of Calvary was first made known in India. Before us lie the ages in which it shall there rule uninterruptedly from sea and sea. What can we do, in our brief life-moment, to hasten that day's coming?

We can begin by taking one of India's 'Regions Beyond'—one sphere where little or no Christian work is done. Probably the most neglected of all its needy districts is BEHAR; at least twenty of whose twenty-four million people are living 'without hope and without GOD.' In 1899, if the Lord will, the BEHAR MISSION will be started.

Will it? And will other equally needed and equally important efforts to reach unevangelised India follow?

I write in faith and hope. The fact depends on you—on you in Australia and Canada, you in the United States and the United Kingdom, you in Germany, France, and Scandinavia, in Switzerland and the Netherlands it may be, you in India itself, perhaps even in Behar, who yet will read these words.

Yes. Will you start these missions? Will you carry them on year by year? Will you give yourself, your children, your means, your influence to one at least of India's 'regions beyond'?

What can you give? What can you do?

How can I tell?

But One can tell you. There is something that you owe Him for India; something that you have not offered yet.

His pierced hand is pointing to the world for which He died. 'Carest thou not?' He whispers.

*　　*　　*　　*　　*

Let us pray.

BEHAR,

a populous region in Northern Bengal, almost as large as England, and with almost as many people, has been lately described by the common consent of leading representatives of the principal Protestant missionary societies working in India, as

'THE MOST NEGLECTED INDIAN MISSION FIELD.'

It contains twenty-four million people (living in twelve great districts running from the frontier of Nepal down to the hot plains of Central India), some of the most fertile lands of India, and is probably the most populous and poorest country on the face of the earth. BEHAR has long been the scene of missionary labour; but, with the exception of four small stations, all the 30 Behar missionaries are working along the main line of the Ganges. At least twenty million people are living beyond the river 'without hope and without God in the world.'

Northern BHAGALPUR, with more than a million people, the whole of SARAN, with two and a half millions, the whole of CHAMPARAN, with 2,000,000; the whole of DHARBANGA, with 2,800,000; the whole of PURNEAH, with 2,000,000; and the great southern district of SHAHABAD, with over 2,000,000 people, have no missionaries at all—to mention only some of the more neglected sections.

The pioneer party of the BEHAR MISSION will, D.V., sail for India in 1899, to commence work, God willing, in one of the great and still wholly unoccupied districts of BEHAR.

Earnest prayer is asked that the Churches may be led forth into a work of faith and labour of love adequate to India's needs. Towards the evangelisation of these long-forgotten millions—as densely heathen as any upon earth—what shall we offer to JESUS CHRIST our LORD?

NOTES

[1] JINANJI JAMSHEDJI MODY, *Parl. of Religions*, vol. ii., p. 906.

[2] *Picturesque India.*

[3] *India and Malaysia.* Bishop Thoburn, pp. 124-6. See also *Hinduism Past and Present.* Dr. Murray Mitchell (R.T.S).

[4] In the 'Cambridge Band' uprising in British Colleges in 1885, and the Student Volunteer Movement, begun at Northfield, Mass., in the summer of 1886.

[5] 'Mohammedan women, if they are pious, pray five times a day. They also fast rigidly during the Ramzan, and weep themselves blind during the Moharram, special mourning services being held in the houses ; but they seldom go to the mosques.

'The religion of Hindu women is obedience to priests and husbands, and superstitious reverence for all the rites, traditions, and customs of their faith. . . . Hinduism is not a religion of love, but of fear. The anger of the gods is dreaded at every step.'—*India and Malaysia*, Thoburn, p. 364.

[6] See *The Land of the Ghauts ; India and Malaysia*, etc.

[7] *Hinduism and Christianity.* John Robson, D.D. (Oliphant, Anderson & Ferrier).

[8] William Carey to Sutcliffe, Smith's *Conversion of India*, pp. 101, 102.

[9] Dr. George Smith's *Conversion of India*, to which masterly work I am indebted for the basis of most of my diagrams.

[10] Bosworth Smith. *Anglican Missionary Conference Report*, 1894, p. 90.

[11] Hyderabad city stands next to Calcutta, Bombay, and Madras, the fourth in population in India. Golconda, of diamond fame, is here ; and Pakhal, the largest lake in India, thirty miles round. For 600 miles of its course the Godavery flows through the single State, more than doubling in one section the whole length of the Thames. The Kistna and Wardha rivers sweep their floods here, giving to Hyderabad alone waterways 150 miles longer than the Thames. But only a tiny streamlet of the river of the water of life has yet been sent to Hyderabad's people. Few parts of India are so little evangelised.

[12] *Our Indian Empire*, Sir Herbert Edwardes. See the Church Missionary Atlas, on *India*, p. 85.

[13] The Rev. Dr. Imad-ud-din . . . gives the names with brief biographies of no fewer than 117 Moslem converts, men of position and influence, of whom 62 became clergy and leading men in several of the Indian missions, and 57 are gentlemen occupying various positions, official and professional.

'It is difficult,' he writes, 'to say how many Mohammedans have become converts, for no separate list is kept . . . now-a-days, there are churches all over India, and in every church there are baptisms from among Mohammedans. . . . There was a time when the conversion of a Mohammedan to Christianity was looked on as a wonder. Now they have come and are coming in their thousands. Compared with converts from amongst Hindus, the converts from amongst Mohammedans are fewer far. . . . Nevertheless, we may thank God that such numbers have become Christians from amongst them, and are now jealous for the faith.'

See C.M.S. *Intelligencer*, Aug., 1893, p. 579.

[14] The eulogists of Hinduism take excellent care, while unveiling the faith of India, to put its repulsive aspects out of view. Professor Lindsay charges Professor Max Müller with being one of the worst offenders in this respect. The German savant who undertook the task of translating the sacred books of the East was confronted in his task with passages so obscene that he could not with any decency reproduce them in his book. While recognising the imperative necessity he was under to eliminate such highly offensive passages, we are still obliged to blame him for maintaining silence as to their existence. Led by this disingenuous guide, the reader sees only the fair side of Hinduism. There is another side—a dark and terrible one, and it is well that this should be remembered to-day when Hinduism would pose as an all-sufficient source of spiritual life to meet not only the wants of the Hindus but even of the world. A glance through the *Yajurveda* would disillusionise anybody. It has been said by the highest legal authority in Bombay that to translate this book would expose the translator to punishment under the Indian Penal Code—indeed, one adventurous individual and his publisher in the Punjab were actually fined for doing so. Professor Max Müller's comparison of Hindu temple women with mediæval nuns earned the contempt of Dr. John Muir—a contempt that will be shared by all who demand truth as the essential element in criticism. Professor Lindsay says :—

'I have seen in a temple a little north of Ahmednuggar the whole wall of a cell covered with large-size pictures of Krishna on a tree with a quantity of women's clothes beside him and a number of perfectly naked women trying to get at their clothes. . . . The Murlis or temple women of Khandoba, a god reverenced over a great part of the Deccan, are married to the god, and part of the marriage vow is to abandon themselves to every pilgrim at the shrine. . . . I was told by a Hindu that the scenes at the pilgrimage time were indescribable, but that they were not so bad now as they once were, because, owing to the spread of Western ideas, men could not now readily believe that acts of the grossest immorality could really be acceptable at divine worship.'—*Extract from an Indian newspaper (condensed)*.

[15] 'Kali, "the black one," is a furious goddess, hideous in features, dripping with blood, gorgon-headed, with a necklace of human skulls, sends pestilence and famine, and is only appeased with blood. In earlier days human sacrifice was often her only propitiation ; and as late as 1866, during the terrible famine, human heads decked with flowers were found before her altar. . . . Her secret cult is too repulsive for description.'—*Picturesque India*, Caine.

[16] Dr. George Smith's *Life of Carey*, p. 64.   [17] Brainerd.   [18] Zinzendorf

ACROSS INDIA AT THE DAWN OF THE 20TH CENTURY

INDEX

Afghan Frontier, 216.
Aggar, The, 213.
Ahmednuggar, 42.
Aitcheson, Sir Charles, 49.
Almora, 217.
American Baptist Missionary Union, 27, 172.
　Board of Missions. 27.
　and English gift to Indian V.M.C.A., 132.
　Presbyterians, 28.
Anantapur, 94.
Anglican Missionary Conference Report, 255 (Note 10).
Appeal, An Unheard, 215.
Appeal for India, Wilder, 5, 32, 215.
Appeal of Bombay Decennial Conference, 210.
Arbuthnot, Mr. Rierson, 131.
Arch of Titus, 13.
Arcot, 150, 152.
Arnold, Sir Edwin. *Light of Asia*, 45, 72.
Assam, 174, 175, 178.
Astor, 215, 217, 246.
Aurungzeeb, 114.
Australian Mission, 28, 43.
Average Missionaries to pop. in Bombay Pres., 28.

Bakharganj, 174, 175, 245.
Balaghat, 152, 154.
Ballia, 217, 245, 251.
Baltistan, 215, 216, 217.
Bania, The, 226, 227.
Basle Missionary Society, 28.
Behar, 175, 176, 177, 246, 251, 253, 254.
　Mission, 253.
Belgaum, 42.
Beluchistan, 41.
Benares, 196, 198, 217.
　Indecent Idols, 198.
Bengal, 174, 175.
Berar, 152, 153.
Berhampore, 175, 176.
Between two Heathendoms, 193.
Bhagavad Gita, 140.
Bhandara, 152, 154.
Bhola, 245.
Bhopal, 152.
Bhotia Buddhist Temple, Prayer Wheel, 191, 192.

Bhotan, 175, 190.
Bible and Tract Society, Madras, 125.
Bishop, Mrs. I. Bird, 242.
Black Hole of Calcutta, 121, 171.
Blackwood, Messrs., 5.
Bogra, 175, 176, 245.
Bombay, 17.
　Commerce, 21.
　Decennial Conference, Appeal of, 210.
　Free Church Mission, 26, 27.
　How it became British, 20.
　Mission, M. E. Church, 26.
　Motto, 21.
　Plague, 22, 23, 26.
　Presidency, unoccupied fields of, 41.
　Average Missionaries to pop., 28.
　Mission Statistics, 28.
　Settlement, 28.
　Towers of Silence, 30.
Bose, Prof. J. C., 139.
Brahmanical Mythology, 80.
Brainerd, 130, 240, 241, 256 (Note 17).
Bride, Hindu, 160.
British and Foreign Bible Society, 5.
Buddhist Prayer, 182.
Burning Ghats, 23, 198.
Burns, William, 240.

Cachar, 175.
　Hills, 178.
Caine, Mr. W. S., 5.
Calcutta, 171, 175.
　Black Hole, 121, 171.
Cambridge Band, 255 (Note 4).
Carey, William, 82, 172, 176, 179.
　Life of Dr. George Smith, 256 (Note 16).
Cashmere, 215, 217.
Catacombs at Rome, 14.
Catechism on Women, Hindu, 162.
　Hindu, 202.
Central Indian Hill Mission, 153.
　Provinces, 152, 153, 246.
Chanda, 152, 153.

Chatterjea, Mr. A., 139.
Chicago, Parliament of Religions, 138.
Child Marriage, 141, 161.
Chillas, 215, 217, 246.
Chitral, 215, 217, 246.
Chota Nagpore, 175, 177.
CHRIST, His Kingdom in India, 27.
　His Passion, 248.
　Misrepresented, 155.
　Waiting for, 209.
Christian College, Madras, 125.
Christian Missions and Social Progress, Dennis, 118.
Christian Vernacular Education Society, 28.
Christlieb, Miss, 94.
Church awaking, 250.
　Missionary Atlas, 255 (Note 12).
　Missionary Society, 5, 27.
　Missionary Society, Divinity School, Madras, 126.
　Missionary Society Intelligencer, 256 (Note 13).
　of Scotland, 5.
　of Scotland Mission, 27, 186, 187.
　Responsible for National Sin, 248.
City of Canterbury, 168.
Clive, Robert, 121.
Coimbatore, 104.
Conference, Indian Student, 50.
Congress, Indian National, 49.
Conjeeveram, 148, 151, 152, 246.
Contents, Table of, 6.
Conversion of India, Dr. G. Smith, 4, 255 (Notes 8 and 9).
Converts from Islam, 119.
Cotton, Sir Arthur, 230.
"Could ye not watch with Me?" 248.

Dacca, 174, 175.
Daily Chronicle, 5.
Darjeeling Railway, 183.
Dawn in India, 79.
Deccan, 43, 181.
Delhi, 112.

R

INDEX

Dennis, *Christian Missions and Social Progress*, 118.
Denny, T. A., Esq., 5.
Dent, Mr. J. M., 5.
Devotees, Hindu, 39.
  of the West, 43.
Diagrams, List of, 9.
Dinajpur, 175.
Dives, 226.
Divorce, Moslem, 119.
Dressmaker, Native, 58.
Duff, Life Work, 236.
Dyer, Mr., 5.

Eddy, Sherwood, 128.
Education, 50.
  of Ramabai's Mother, 85.
Education, Want of, for Women, 208.
Educational Statistics, 49.
Edwardes, Sir Herbert, 255 (Note 12).
Emmerson, 35.
England, Work for Women in, 68.
Elliot, 240.
Estimated Cost of Famine of '97, 226.
Etawah, 217.
Ethics of Islam, Dr. Post, 108.
Everest, Mount, 183.

Faith Mission (Mr. and Mrs. Innes-Wright), 187.
Fakirs, 36, 198.
Famine Corpse, 225.
  Estimated Cost of, 226.
  Experiences, Ramabai, 89.
  Hospital, 224.
  Poorhouse, 222.
  Sufferers (Indian girls), 90.
Faridpore, 176.
Farrar, *Witness of History to CHRIST*, 138.
Fatipur, 217.
Ferozepore, 217, 219.
First Protestant Missionaries to India, 130.
Flags, Prayer, 189.
Floods on the dry ground, 234.
Free Church Mission, Bombay, 26, 27.
Free Church of Scotland, 5.

Gangpur, 178.
Gardiner, Allen, 240.
Gethsemane, 248.
Ghauts, The Land of the, 255 (Note 6).
Ghauts, Western, 47.
Gilgit, 215, 217, 246.
Girls' Schools in India, 68.
Gladstone, 166.
Godavery, Irrigation Works, 229.

GOD's protest against His prophets, 242.
Gordon, Dr. A. J., 180.
Govind, 55.
Govindgar, 212.
Guinness, Dr., Lectures in Poona, 56.
Gunputti, 72, 77.

Hannuman, 76.
Harris, Lord, 20.
Havelock, Sir Arthur, 130.
Hazara, 216, 217.
Heathen Mother's Influence, 66.
Hewlett, Miss, 224.
Heywood, Mr. and Mrs., 48.
Hill Tipperah, 178.
Hindu Bride, 160.
  Catechism, 202.
  Catechism on Women, 162.
  Devotees, 39.
  Education, 50.
  Funeral, 22.
  Philosophy, its Fruit, 145.
  Wedding, 157.
  Widowhood, 87.
  Widow's Prayer, 163.
  Women, 202, 255 (Note 5).
  Worship, 77.
Hinduism, 146, 256 (Note 14).
  Abomination worship, 79.
Hinduism and Christianity, John Robson, 255 (Note 7).
Hinduism Denies Existence of Sin, 139.
  Doctrine of Salvation, 36, 37.
Hinduism's Holy of Holies, 195.
  Methods of Purging Sin, 197.
Hinduism Past and Present, Murray Mitchell, 255 (Note 3).
  —330,000,000 gods, 73.
  Transmigration Theory, 40.
Hinkley, Mr. and Mrs., 94.
Home for Indian Widows, Ramabai's, 86.
Hoshangabad, 152.
Hunza, 215, 217, 246.
Hurda, 152.
Hydembad, 105, 246, 251, 255 (Note 11).

Idolatry, 141, 150.
Idols, Indecent, Benares, 198.
"If—," 214, 243, 246, 248.
Illustrations, List of, 7, 8.
Imad-ud-din, the Rev. Dr., 255 (Note 13).
Imrah Patta, 212.
Indecent Idols, Benares, 198.
India and Malaysia, Bishop Thoburn, 255 (Notes 3 and 5).

India Office, 5.
Indian Female Normal Schools, 28.
  Girls, 68.
  Girls—Famine Sufferers, 90.
  National Congress, 49.
  Penal Code vetos parts of Hindu Scriptures, 147.
  Student Conferences, 50.
India's Rivers, 228.
  Women, 61-64, 141.
Indore, 152, 153.
Innes-Wright, Mr. and Mrs., 187.
Introduction, 10-15.
Irrigation Results in Madras, 121.
  Works, Godavery, 229.
  Works, their value, 231.
Irish Presbyterians, 28.
Islam, Immorality of, 243.
  Spirit and Teaching of, 111.

Jain Temple at Poona, 82.
Jaisalmir, 217, 220.
Jami Musjid, 112.
Jasmine Tower (Saman Burj), 143.
Jhalsapatam, 217, 220.
Jhelum, 217, 219.
Jinanji Jamshedji Mody, 255 (Note 1).
Jubilee Procession, Cost of, 226.
Judgment Impending Unperceived, 243.
Judson, 172.
  Life Work, 237.

Kaaba, Mecca, 115, 244.
Kaffiristan, 212, 215, 217, 246.
Kalahandi State, 152.
Kali, 72, 79, 171, 174, 256 (Note 15).
Kalighat, 171.
Kanker State, 152.
Karens, 172.
Karma, 40.
Kashin Hills, 175, 178.
Kathiawar, 42, 43.
Khandeish, 42.
Kinchinjanga, 188, 189.
Kipling, Rudyard, 17, 58, 157.
Kistiwar Province, 215, 217, 246.
Kistna, South, 152.
Kohat, 216, 217.
Kollegal, 104.
Kolhapur, 42, 43.
Koran, The, 116.
  Sanctions Immorality, 243.
Krishna, 79, 256 (Note 14).
Kurku and Central India Hill Mission, 152.
Kurrachee, 41.
Kutch, 41, 42, 245.
Kwanyin, 84.

INDEX

259

Ladak, 215, 216.
Lal Bazaar Baptist Chapel, 172.
Land of the Ghauts, 255 (Note 6).
Lee, Mr. James, 5.
Leh, Moravian Missions, 215.
Lepcha, 193.
Lepcha Bearers, 183.
Life of Carey, Dr. George Smith, 256 (Note 16).
Light of Asia, Sir Edwin Arnold, 45.
Lindsay, Professor, 256 (Note 14).
Livingstone, 240.
London Missionary Society, 5, 28.
  Missionary Society Famine Work, 222.
  Mission House, 94.
Lone Star Mission, 150, 172.
Luther, 14, 238.
Lyall, Sir James, 232.

Macaulay, 50, 80, 195.
Macklean, Dr. and Mrs., 26.
Madras, 107, 120, 125, 126, 152.
  Irrigation Results, 121.
  Missionary Conference, 128.
  Missions, 150.
  Mission Staff, 125.
  Observatory, 166.
  Presidency, 150, 152.
  Presidency, population of, 123.
  Scotch Kirk, 125.
  Students, 142.
  Y.M.C.A., 130.
Madura, 152.
Mahatmas, 140.
Malabar Hill, 17, 30.
Maldah, 175, 178, 245.
Malvalli, 104.
Mandla, 152, 153.
Manipur, 175, 178, 245.
Manu, 62, 202.
Marrat, Mr., 80.
Maruti, 75.
McConaghy, Mr. D., 131.
Mecca, Kaaba, 115, 244.
Meher Daver, 31.
Menzies, Mrs., 5.
Methodist Episcopal Missions, 28.
Midnapur, 175, 176.
Mission Work, Mysore, 105.
Missionary Conference, Madras, 128.
Missionary Review of the World, 239.
Missions in Madras, 150.
Mitchell, Dr. Murray, 255 (Note 3).
Mody, Jinanji Jamshedji, 255 (Note 1).
Moffat, Robert, 237.

Mohammedan Divorce, 119.
  Map of the World, 116.
  Women, 255 (Note 5).
Mohomet and his Wives, 119.
Montenegro, 153.
Moravian Mission Founders, 241.
  Missions, Leh., 215.
Morley, Miss, 137.
Moslems compelled to Religious Toleration, 119.
  Under British Rule, 111.
Mott, Mr. John R., 44, 49, 52.
Muller, Max, *Sacred Books of the East*, 147, 256 (Note 14).
Murray, Mitchell, Dr., *Hinduism Past and Present*, 255 (Note 3).
Mymensing, 175, 176.
Mysore, 41, 104, 105, 152, 246.
Mythology, Brahmanical, 80.

Nadiyah, 175, 176.
Naga Hills, 178.
Nagpore, 152.
Nanga Parbut, 215.
Native Dressmaker, 58.
Native States, Punjab, 245.
Native Theatre, Poona, 48.
Negapatam, 150.
Neo-Hinduism, 139, 141.
Nepal, 76, 190, 217.
Nestorian Church, 123.
  Tablet, N. China, 124.
  Travancore, 124.
Neve, Drs. (C.M.S.), 215.
Nizam's Dominions, 105, 152.
North Nellore District, 152.
North West Provinces, 217, 220.
Notes, 255.
Nur Mahal, 114.

Observatory, Madras, 166.
Orlebar, Miss, 134.
Oudh, 217, 220.
Our Indian Empire, 255 (Note 12).

Pabna, 175.
Palaman, 175, 177.
Palamcotta, 150.
Parbutti Temple, Poona, 74, 75.
Parliament of Religions, 138, 255 (Note 1).
Parsee Hotel, 46.
  Ladies, 32.
Parsees, 20, 30, 32.
Patient, Thomas, 103.
Patnakali, 245.
Paton, 238, 240, 241.
Pearl Mosque at Delhi, 112.
Persia, 243.
Peshawar, 216, 217.

Picturesque India, 255 (Note 2), 256 (Note 14).
Plague in Bombay, 22, 23, 25.
Poona, 42, 44.
  Native Theatre, 48.
  Shrines of, 75.
  Parbutti Temple, 74, 75.
  Jain Temple, 82.
Post, Dr., *Ethics of Islam*, 108.
Post Office, Calcutta, 171.
Prayer Flags, 189.
  Rags, 182.
  Wheel, 182, 192.
Preface, 4.
Protestant Missionaries to India, First, 130.
Punch State, 215, 217, 246.
Punjab, 217, 218, 232, 245.

Raipore, 152, 153.
Rajkote, 42.
Rajputana, 217, 220.
Rama, Death Song, 22.
Ramabai, 61, 143.
  Famine Experiences, 149.
  Home for Indian Widows, 86.
  Life Story, 87.
  Parentage, 85.
Rampore Bolia, 175, 176.
Ranee, 200.
Ranjitsinjhi, 139.
Rawal Pindi, 216.
Regions Beyond Forward Movement, 252.
Religions of India, Macaulay, 80.
Religious Tract Society, 5.
Rivers of Living Water, 234.
Robson, Dr., 80, 255 (Note 7).
Route of Tour, 4.

Sacred Books of the East, Max Muller, 147.
Salvation Army, 28, 125, 126, 127.
Saman Burj (Jasmine Tower), 143.
Santa Scala, 14.
Satturn, 42.
Scandinavian Alliance, 187.
Schools for Girls, India, 68.
Scotch Kirk, Madras, 125.
Seharanpore, 217.
Senchal, 184.
Shan Jehan, Pearl Mosque of, 114.
Sialkote, 217, 219, 245.
Sikkim, 188, 189.
Sind, 41, 42.
Siva, 72, 77, 79, 174.
Smith, Dr. George, 5, 101
  Conversion of India, 4, 255 (Notes 8 and 9).

INDEX

Smith *Students' Geography of India*, 153.
   Mr. Bosworth, 255 (Note 10).
   Life of Carey, 256. (Note 16.)
Society for the Propagation of the Gospel, 27.
   for Suppression of Opium Traffic, 5.
South American Mission, 240.
   Sea races, 241.
Speer, Robert E., 243.
Spence, Miss (L.M.S.), 5, 204.
Spiritual Life in Y.M.C.A., India, 132, 133.
Spurgeon, Rev. C. H., 120.
Statistics, Educational, 49.
   Missions, Bombay Presidency, 28.
   Women of India, 165.
Stanley, 238.
Stock, Eugene, Esq., 5.
Student Conferences, Indian, 50.
   Movement (India and Ceylon), 5, 50.
   Volunteer Movement, 255 (Note 4).
Students' Geography of India, Dr. G. Smith, 153.
Students, Indian, 50.
   Madras, 142.
Sun-worshippers, 32.
Sunday School Union, 5, 128.
Suniassis, 198.
Swami Vivekenanda, *see* Vivekenanda.

Table of Contents, 6.
Taglak, 113.
Taj Mahal, 114.
Tamasha, 158.
Tamerlane, 113.
Tanjore, 152.

Taylor, Miss Annie, 185.
Telegu Churches, 28.
   Country, 150.
   Lone Star Mission, 172.
Temple Women, 256 (Note 14).
Thibet, 185, 189, 217.
Thibetan Pioneer Mission, 186.
Thoburn, Bishop, 5, 39, 79, 116, 119.
   Bishop, *India and Malaysia*, 255 (Notes 3 and 5).
Tiger Hill, 183.
Times of India, The, 20.
Tinnevelly, 150.
Tipperâh, 175.
Titus, Arch of, 13.
Tonk, 217, 220.
Towers of Silence, 32.
   Bombay, 30.
Tract and Book Societies, 27.
Transmigration Theory, 39, 40.
Travancore, 150, 152.
   Nestorian Tablet, 124.

Uganda, First Missionaries to, 239.
Unwin, Mr. Fisher, 5.

Vishnu, 77.
Vivekenanda, 138, 147, 155, 161.

Wadhwan, 42.
Waiting for CHRIST, 209.
Walkeshwar, 35.
Want of Education for Women.
Ward, Mr. and Mrs. (L.M.S.), 125.
Wardha, 152, 154.
Wedding, Hindu, 157.
Wesley, John, his Life Work, 235.
Westcott, Bishop, 119.
Wheat, Water Carriage of, 231.
Whitefield, his Life Work, 235.

Whittier, 211.
Widowhood, 87, 162.
Wilder, Robert P., Account of Student Convert (Govind), 54, 55.
   Appeal for India, 5, 32.
Williams, his Life Work, 236.
Witness of History to CHRIST. Farrar, 138.
Women, Hindu idea of, 202.
   Indian, Illiteracy of, 64.
   Indian, Number of, 64.
   Mohammedan, 255 (Note 5).
Women of India, 141, 200, 203.
   Statistics, 165.
   Suffering, 161.
   Want of Education, 208.
Woolmer, Miss, 5.
Workers wanted in India, Y.W.C.A., 137.
World's Student Christian Federation, 54.

Yajurveda, 147.
Yogi, 140.
Yogis, 198.
Young Men's Christian Association, 28, 132, 133.
   Madras, 130.
   American and English gift to, 132.
Young Women's Christian Association, 125, 137.
   Annual Expenditure in India, 137.
   Calcutta, 134.
   in India, 133.

Zenana Bible and Medical Mission, 5.
   Visiting, 208.
   Work, 28, 60.
Zinzendorf, 241, 256 (Note 18.)
Zoroastrianism, 31.

STATISTICAL BASIS

The figures for population used in this book are quoted from the last census—that of 1891, with the exception of the populations of the provinces and presidencies—Bombay, Madras, Bengal, Punjab, North-West Provinces, etc., for which an estimate enlarged for the close of the century has been employed.

Mr. Maurice Gregory has carefully worked out this enlarged estimate, basing his calculations for each presidency separately on the growth of the population between the last two censuses.

www.ingramcontent.com/pod-product-compliance
Lightning Source LLC
Chambersburg PA
CBHW021357230426
43666CB00006B/556